ÆDES CHRISTI
in Academia Oxoniensi

A KING'S BOOK OF KINGS

STUART CARY WELCH

A KING'S BOOK OF KINGS

THE SHAH-NAMEH OF SHAH TAHMASP

Published by

THAMES AND HUDSON
LONDON

In association with

THE METROPOLITAN MUSEUM
OF ART, NEW YORK

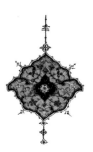

All photography, pages 78-187, by Malcolm Varon, New York
Book designed by Peter Oldenburg
Composition by Finn Typographic Service Inc.
Printed in Switzerland by Imprimeries Réunies S.A. Lausanne
Bound in Switzerland by Mayer & Soutter, Renens
Production supervision by Helvetica Press Incorporated, New York
Published in Great Britain, 1972, by Thames and Hudson Limited
ISBN: 0 500 23178 8

Contents

On behalf of the Government of Iran, may I say how delighted we are that The Metropolitan Museum of Art is publishing this important book on the celebrated "Houghton *Shah-nameh*," written and illustrated for Shah Tahmasp in the second quarter of the sixteenth century. Because this manuscript is one of the jewels of Iranian art, it is especially appropriate that it is now being made known to a large public. No Islamic volume of the time has a more complete set of colorful, carefully executed miniatures painted by great court artists. Through the combined efforts of the Metropolitan Museum, the Chairman of the Board, Arthur A. Houghton, Jr., the President, the Honorable Douglas Dillon, and all the Trustees, together with the distinguished direction of Thomas Hoving, the guidance of Richard Ettinghausen, Consultative Chairman of the Department of Islamic Art, the excellent scholarship of Stuart Cary Welch and his associate Martin Bernard Dickson, and with assistance from the Iran-America Society, the project has become not only a reality but a resounding success.

By this scholarly achievement The Metropolitan Museum has honored the 2500th Anniversary of the Founding of the Persian Empire by Cyrus the Great, and also the first Declaration of Human Rights. Since the *Shah-nameh,* our national epic, relates the early history of our country down to the seventh century, we feel that this forms a natural educational introduction to the significance of our great Anniversary for the American people. We are extremely pleased that in addition a special exhibition and a film on the same subject will make the many visitors to the Museum fully aware of the glories of Iranian art.

Ever since the founding of the Museum, Iranian art has been given an outstanding place in its collections, and many beautiful examples of our national heritage have been displayed to full advantage. We are very pleased to see our art exhibited so prominently in the United States, and now, thanks to the Museum's remarkable efforts, your public will have an additional opportunity to become further acquainted with Iranian history.

As President of the Western Hemisphere Committees, whose United States Committee is headed by Mrs. Richard M. Nixon, Honorary Chairman, and Ralph E. Becker, General Chairman, I congratulate the Museum for this outstanding publication. Such works assist greatly in bringing about an even closer relationship between the people of Iran and the United States, two peoples dedicated to the principles of freedom, morality, and tolerance set forth by Cyrus the Great so many years ago.

Amir Aslan Afshar
Ambassador of Iran to the United States of America

Foreword

FOR THE museum man there are, quite irrespective of period and place of origin, two general groups of objects. One is comprised of monumental works: architectural components, large sculptures, altarpieces, carpets, tapestries. Often very striking, these are certainly the eye-catching objects in the galleries. The other group is represented by small portable objects, often of a de luxe nature: devotional pictures, pieces of jewelry, manuscripts. Objects of this group need a closer scrutiny to be fully understood and appreciated, but then their exquisite workmanship, refinement, and many subtle aspects all join to provide a truly thrilling experience. It sometimes happens that the art of an entire period is focused in just such a small marvel of creation. When a particular work of art crystallizes an entire epoch for us, physical size ceases to matter.

Iranian painting—which means specifically miniature painting in books—has always been regarded as one of the most original and exquisite forms of the pictorial arts, and indeed its style is unique. Were one to look for an art object to epitomize Iranian art and provide the ideal artistic experience that only a true masterpiece can give, one could find none better than the manuscript known today as the Houghton *Shah-nameh*. Prepared for a king during one of the greatest periods of Iranian art, it is clearly one of the finest Islamic manuscripts ever created. It seems wonderfully appropriate that this manuscript should serve as the Metropolitan Museum's offering in saluting the Iranian people in celebration of the 2500th anniversary of their great country—a country that has always played an important role in history and has ever been in the vanguard of the human endeavor to expand the range and heighten the quality of cultural achievements. Our showing of the choicest paintings to be found in the manuscript is a very special artistic privilege, heightened further because it is offered by a most loyal friend of the Museum, Arthur A. Houghton, Jr., Chairman of the Board of Trustees. Not only has he made our exhibition possible, he has very generously presented to the Museum seventy-eight of the book's miniatures, a group that represents its wide artistic range.

WE ARE grateful to Stuart Cary Welch, Curator of Indian and Islamic Painting, Fogg Art Museum, Harvard University, for the present informative account of the Houghton *Shah-nameh,* which he consented to write at the request of Richard Ettinghausen, Consultative Chairman of the Museum's Department of Islamic Art. Long a student of Islamic art, Mr. Welch is particularly qualified for his task because he has studied the manuscript for years, preparing a major publication on it in collaboration with Martin Bernard Dickson of Princeton University. Publication of the present book has been made possible in part by funds provided by His Excellency Dr. Amir Aslan Afshar, the Ambassador of Iran in Washington, on behalf of the Imperial Government of Iran. I also mention gratefully the helpful role played by Ralph E. Becker, President of the Iran-America Society.

THOMAS HOVING

Acknowledgments

THIS BOOK, a greatly condensed version of a study that will eventually be published by Harvard University Press, could not have been written without the help of many friends. The most helpful of all has been Martin Bernard Dickson of Princeton University, an outstanding scholar of the Safavid period and my collaborator in the larger project. Even before we began our work on the Houghton manuscript we had concluded that Safavid painting was not (as had been supposed previously) a direct continuation of the Herat style of Bihzad. Rather, we had seen it as stemming from other sources as well, particularly from the little-known but equally significant artistic style of Turkman Tabriz. Study of the Houghton *Shah-nameh* has greatly reinforced this belief for us. Without the generously shared knowledge of Professor Dickson, I could not have supported my arguments with historical and literary evidence—nor would I know as much as I do now about the tying of turbans, say, or painter Dust Muhammad's addiction to wine.

I am also greatly indebted to the late Eric Schroeder, Curator of Islamic Art at the Fogg Museum and the most brilliant mind I know of in the field of Iranian painting; he listened to me patiently and looked carefully with me over many years. John Rosenfield, more than anyone else, read critically what I wrote and gave me consistently wise counsel. John Coolidge, with whom the study began, has shown a stoic devotion to our continuing work, as has Arthur A. Houghton, Jr., whose acquisition of the manuscript set the whole thing in motion. Basil W. Robinson accepted my radical ideas about the origins of Safavid art even before I had seen the Houghton manuscript, and it was he who informed me of the *Guy u Chawgan* manuscript in Leningrad. Also, it was he who identified several of the strayed pages from the British Museum's *Khamseh* of Nizami. Above all, he most generously lent me his extraordinarily informative notes on most of the major collections and libraries in the days when I first seriously studied Iranian painting. Another I should like to thank is Philip Hofer; his friendly encouragement sustained me in dark moments. Other scholars whose work has been enlightening are: Ivan Stchoukine, whose orderly and perceptive study of virtually all of Islamic painting continues to be a loving labor; Basil Gray, whose areas of creative connoisseurship have included valuable excursions into the Iranian field; and Richard Ettinghausen, not only generous and helpful but responsible for the idea of my writing this curtailed version of the larger book.

At various times and in many different ways the following have been especially helpful: Ralph Pinder-Wilson, G. M. Meredith-Owens, Mme T. Greck, Anatoli Ivanov, Uri Borshevskii, M. Bayani, J. V. S. Wilkinson, and Sir Chester Beatty; also Robert Skelton, Amin Bayani, Roy Mottahedeh, Dorothy Miner, Marie L. Swietochowski, Mildred Frost, and Sally Walker; also Anthony Welch and Milo Cleveland Beach, known as my students, but in fact my notably generous colleagues and friends.

Above all, I express gratitude to the artists who long ago created the Houghton *Shah-nameh,* especially to Sultan Muhammad. When I began this study, it was to learn about art; in the end I had learned about life.

S.C.W.

A KING'S BOOK OF KINGS

IT IS A HEAVY BOOK, almost too big to handle, intended for special occasions, portentous but entertaining. The smooth binding is warmly, solidly patinated by time and handling. The cover opens like a massive, well-oiled door. The dry, mellowed pages, thin but firm, crackle pleasantly as one turns them.

A copy of Iran's national epic, the *Shah-nameh (Book of Kings),* composed by the poet Firdowsi in the tenth century, was practically a part of any Iranian ruler's regalia—usually along with a poem extolling the king himself. Several *Shah-nameh* manuscripts commissioned by kings have survived, but none is grander in scale or contents than the example to be discussed here. Its two hundred and fifty-eight figurative paintings, its splendid illuminations, and its rich binding make the Houghton *Shah-nameh,* identified by the name of its present owner, the most sumptuous of all. Furthermore, because of the scarcity of surviving buildings, textiles, and other examples of the decorative arts of the time, this book is perhaps the most impressive extant monument of sixteenth-century Iranian culture. No other major royal manuscript of the first half of the sixteenth century now has more than fourteen contemporary miniatures; this one, by contrast, is virtually a portable art gallery. In it one can trace the evolution of Safavid painting through the formative early 1520s to its maturity in the mid-1530s and beyond. Most of the illustrious court artists of the period contributed to the book. Several of these men have been little more than names to us until now. In almost every case, known works by them were so rare that it was difficult if not impossible to gain much understanding of their styles. Studying the Houghton manuscript, we not only identify more of their work but follow their evolutions as painters during a time of dramatic changes and thus understand the formation of the Safavid civilization with fresh insight.

The manuscript contains few hints as to its history. The text ends abruptly on folio 759 recto, with neither a date nor the name of the scribe. Near the beginning, a rosette with cartouches (reproduced on page 78) is inscribed with the name and praises of Shah Tahmasp, the second Safavid ruler, the man for whom the manuscript was written and illustrated. As we shall see, the volume was probably commissioned in 1522 by the founder of the Safavid dynasty, Shah Isma'il, as a gift for his young son, then Prince Tahmasp, who that year, aged nine, returned to the capital, Tabriz, from Herat. Shah Tahmasp's name occurs a second time in the book, discreetly inscribed above a fortress gateway in the miniature on folio 442 verso. The only date written in the book, 934 A.H., corresponding to A.D. 1527/28, occurs on folio 516 verso, on an architectural panel (page 169). As this miniature appears late in the book, the date was likely written several years after work on the commission was begun.

Only two of the manuscript's two hundred and fifty-eight figurative paintings are inscribed with the names of their painters. One of these, on folio 60 verso, contains the name Mir Musavvir, who was one of the leading court painters, written in tiny characters on the hat of a small figure in the crowded composition. The other name appears beneath a painting that was added ten or fifteen years after the completion of the bulk of the project (page 173). The name is Dust Muhammad, and he is almost certainly the scribe and artist whose work as a miniaturist is otherwise known only in unpublished material in the Topkapu Seray Museum, Istanbul. Though Dust Muhammad was a notable calligrapher as well as painter, his more recent renown comes from his comments on paintings and painters in an album of miniatures, drawings, and calligraphies he assembled for Bahram Mirza, a brother of Shah Tahmasp. This "account of past and present painters," written in 1546 and now in the Topkapu Seray Library, is one of the most valuable of art-historical discussions. In it there is a reference to a painting by Sultan Muhammad, who was called the "Zenith of the Age," showing "people clothed in leopard skins," which was "in a *Shah-nameh* of the shah [and] was such that the hearts of the boldest painters were grieved and they hung their heads in shame before it." When Arthur Houghton and I first turned the pages of his *Shah-nameh* it was this painting we looked for, to know if the volume was indeed the great and legendary *Shah-nameh* noted by Dust Muhammad. Our anticipations were realized when we reached folio 20 verso and faced perhaps the greatest painting in Iranian art (page 89).

Dust Muhammad, associated with our manuscript both as illustrator and historian, also mentions two other artists, Aqa Mirak and Mir Musavvir, "Sayyids [who] painted in the royal library, illustrating a *Shah-nameh* and a *Khamseh* so beautifully that the pen is inadequate to describe their merits." It is almost certain that he is speaking again of the Houghton *Shah-nameh* and a now fragmentary *Khamseh* in the British Museum. Though it is dated 1539 to 43, the *Khamseh,* according to Dust Muhammad, was still unfinished in 1544. We shall return to this *Khamseh* later, in considering some final points about the *Shah-nameh.*

Inasmuch as all librarians' and owners' seals and commentaries have vanished from the Houghton manuscript—if they ever existed—the manuscript's peregrinations from the time when Dust Muhammad's inscribed miniature was added (probably around 1540) until 1800 are uncertain. However, its extraordinarily fresh condition, showing few ill effects from damp, insects, or the many other hazards of Eastern libraries, proves that it was always treated with due regard. In 1800 it was in the Royal Ottoman Library, Istanbul, where a synopsis of the action was written on a protective sheet covering each miniature. These synopses were added by Muhammad Arifi, a librarian in the service of the Turkish sultan Selim III (1789–1807). How did the manuscript reach the Ottoman capital? As a gift? As booty from one of the Ottoman invasions of Iran? Conceivably it was part of a lavish accession present—known to have included such a manuscript—which was sent to Sultan Murad III by Shah Tahmasp in 1576, the year of Shah Tahmasp's death.

In 1903 the manuscript appeared in Paris, when it was one of the major items in an exhibition of Islamic art at the Musée des Arts Decoratifs. The lender was Baron Edmond de Rothschild. Although the manuscript has been in Europe or America ever since, it was not included in the major exhibitions of Islamic art in Munich (1910), Paris (1912), London (1931), or New York (1940). Since its acquisition in 1959 by Arthur A. Houghton, Jr., miniatures from it have been in exhibitions at the Grolier Club (1962), M. Knoedler and Company (1968), the Pierpont Morgan Library (1968), and the Asia House Gallery (1970).

Even though it was seen by few people for half a century after 1903, the manuscript was often in the minds of those concerned with the Islamic book. Its first published notice was the catalogue listing of the 1903 exhibition, compiled by Gaston Migeon, Max van Berchem, and Charles Huart. Since this information contains errors that were afterward repeated as part of the "legend" of the book, it may be well to call attention to them:

> No. 823 Manuscrit, Le Schah Nameh, composé vers l'an 1000 de l'ère par ordre du Sultan Mahmud le Geznévide. Ecrit en l'année 944 [sic] de l'Hégire 1566 [sic] par le scribe et artiste Kacem Esriri [sic]; et offert au Sultan de Perse Thamasp Ier de la dynastie des Sofis à Ispahan (1524–1574), en même temps qu'Akbar régnait sur les Mongoles à Delhi.

As noted earlier, the only date to be found in the manuscript is 934 A.H. The erroneous 944, moreover, is wrongly calculated as 1566; it should be 1537. Further, the "scribe and artist" Kacem Esriri would seem to owe the fiction of his existence to a misreading. And of course Shah Tahmasp died in 1576, not 1574.

At the time of the exhibition Gaston Migeon and Edgard Blochet wrote enthusiastic notices of the *Shah-nameh,* Migeon acclaiming it as "the most precious book here . . . [with] few equals anywhere." As none of the paintings was again shown publicly until 1962, students of Persian painting who were not fortunate enough to be granted a private viewing could consider the manuscript only on the basis of a small and inadequate series of reproductions of its miniatures. A few of these appeared in Migeon's review of the exhibition and one was reproduced in his *Manuel d'art Musulman* (1907). Others were published by F. R. Martin, a Swedish bon vivant, diplomat, collector, scholar, and sometime dealer, in his pioneering study, *The Miniature Painting and Painters of Persia, India, and Turkey from the 8th to the 18th Century* (1912). Although Martin was a connoisseur of distinction and his book is still an essential one for the specialist, his selection of miniatures from this manuscript was deplorable, as was his discussion of it. His comments and plates in fact make one wonder whether he ever actually saw the manuscript—or if he disliked its owner. Another writer on the manuscript was Sir Thomas Arnold, and his specific and appreciative comments about it in *The Islamic Book* (1929) lead one to think he examined the *Shah-nameh* seriously. Other mentions of the manuscript in the standard books on Persian painting were based on Martin's inadequate selection of illustrations, and few of these authors avoided being influenced by Martin's unaccountable underestimation of the manuscript's quality.

The Making of the Book

CERTAIN STEPS can be assumed in the creation of any Islamic manuscript. First must come the idea—in this case a grand one—then the people and materials to implement it. Presumably Shah Isma'il himself authorized this particularly vast project, so the royal workshops, with their corps of skilled craftsmen and artists, were available. Men and materials from all over Iran and beyond had to be mustered for a book of such magnificence, which only a great ruler could have afforded—and which, of course, proclaimed the might of the patron. Before the actual work could proceed, a director was needed to act as intermediary between the patron and his legion of workmen, and to inspire the workmen with the highest standards. In this instance Sultan Muhammad, the greatest Safavid artist, may well have held the appointment, for his personality is stamped upon the earliest pictures in the book, many of which he painted or designed. If he was not actually in charge of the project, he was certainly the moving force behind its illustrations.

The director's first task was to assemble the paper, inks, gold and silver leaf, pigments, brushes, leather for the bindings, and glues—to mention only the more obvious among the manifold articles required. In Safavid Iran even this much must have been a complex task. Consider the paper alone. As Iranian books did not conform to standard sizes, the thin, sturdy sheets had to be made especially. And inasmuch as the border areas of each page are flecked with gold, a process carried out on the wet paper prior to sizing and burnishing, the areas for the paintings and text had to be decided in advance. Once gilded, sized, and burnished, the paper was brought to the director, who by now presumably had laid out the schema for at least the first portion of the book.

As one can see by glancing at the manuscript's first thirty or so folios, the format of each illustrated page was individually conceived. The spacing depended on such factors as the number of verses to be included, the number of columns of text to the page, the episode to be illustrated, the balance of the page in relation to the facing one, and the planner's invariable desire to make the turning of each folio a delight. The layout of the many illustrated pages—almost every folio through the first eighty-five and beyond—must have been particularly challenging. Since the writing of the text ordinarily preceded its illustration, as can be seen from places where an artist's pigments cover the scribe's ink, the director, probably in consultation with the patron, had not only to decide which subjects were to be depicted but what their spatial requirements would be. Conceivably, he sketched in some of the designs for the miniatures at this juncture, along with notations as to the disposition of the columns of text.

The director then submitted the pages to the scribe, who began the demanding process of writing out Firdowsi's sixty thousand or so verses, together with the introduction to them written for Prince Baysunghur, the Timurid bibliophile for whom a magnificent *Shah-nameh* had been completed nearly a century before, in 1430. The task of copying Firdowsi's verses, to suggest a comparison, was greater than if the scribe had been required to copy the King James Bible. In relation to Iranian art, however, "copying" is too workaday a term. In Islamic countries calligraphy was—and still is—a major art, and scribes were esteemed at least as much as painters.

After the scribe had written the first part of the book, the pages were returned to the director, who no doubt checked them carefully before passing them on to the painters. Sultan Muhammad—assuming that he was the director—kept several to paint himself, sending others to artists within his immediate circle, most of whom worked under the master's close supervision or even with his direct participation. Certain of the pages may well have been given at this point to other high-ranking painters, such as Aqa Mirak or Mir Musavvir, some of whose paintings appear early in the book, though they were not necessarily painted in the early stages of the project.

The chronology inherent in the manuscript is complex. Certain of the pictures near the beginning, such as *Firdowsi's parable of the ship of Shi'ism* (page 85), can be seen, on the basis of style, to have been painted when the project was well advanced. Conceivably, such paintings replaced earlier, less admired paintings. At least one of the first pictures in the book, Sultan Muhammad's *The court of Gayumars* (page 89), was begun early but must have required several years to complete.

Assignments of the pages were made according to the artists' talents. Mir Musavvir, for instance, specialized in pretty girls and handsome youths. He was adept at romantic themes, and several of these were given to him (page 169). An unidentifiable artist, called by us Painter E, was chosen for active outdoor subjects. Battle scenes, present in the book nearly to the point of monotony, were well suited to E's predilection for leaping horses, athletic heroes, and glittering gold and silver panoplies. He was assigned these in quantity, along with other subjects unlikely to have inspired artists of less martial temperament. In Iranian art unpleasant episodes were often overlooked; when they could not be avoided the task of illustrating them was apt to be given to a painter whose pictures could be ignored. Thus, the disagreeable chore of depicting the tragic death of the central hero, Rustam, was foisted upon Painter E, and he distinguished himself in so unexciting and archaic a fashion that one can skim over the scene without shedding a tear.

Sultan Muhammad's guidance of the project ended well before its completion. However, regardless of his departure from the project, the impact of his style carries through the manuscript (as it does, indeed, through all later Safavid painting). Mir Musavvir seems to have been the next director. His influence upon the same lesser artists who had previously worked with Sultan Muhammad becomes intense after the first hundred or more folios. Another unidentified hand, Painter C, can be seen to have had this master's help in several miniatures. Unlike Sultan Muhammad, Mir Musavvir seems to have had difficulty in leading his followers. His graceful, hard edged forms and immaculately brilliant palette were beyond the potential of such artists as Painter C, an old man, set in his ways, whose bee-sting formula for mouths makes it easy to identify his work. One can envision scenes between the master and the assistant in which Mir Musavvir, unable to turn what to him must have been a sow's ear into a silk purse, satisfied himself by adding a few masterly strokes of the brush. If the silk purse was not possible, at least he could attach a small jewel to the ear.

Still later, Aqa Mirak became the leading force in the project. The same lesser painters who had served the previous directors now became his followers. As one might expect, these artists (Painters A, B, C, D, E, F) took on stylistic elements of the third director's manner while remaining fundamentally true to their own styles, upon which traces remained of those of Sultan Muhammad and Mir Musavvir. Though at times the mixture is a bit baffling, it is ultimately possible to sort out the hands and influences.

While we cannot here discuss the artistic personalities and developments of each of the artists, it is important to be aware of their differences and to know something of their roles. Another of the senior painters, Dust Muhammad, although he never became director, joined the corps of illustrators with a picture on folio 308 verso. He painted five of his six miniatures for the book during the years of the actual production, adding the sixth some time later.

While the senior artists worked on, younger artists grew up and became masters. Five such can be identified: Mirza Ali, Mir Sayyid Ali, Muzaffar Ali, Shaykh Muhammad, and Abd al-Samad. Although a few of their pictures would seem to have been painted when they were perhaps still in their teens, their best pictures for the manuscript rank among their finest anywhere. Mirza Ali, who was Sultan Muhammad's son, was honored as a very young man by being invited to paint the third miniature in the book (page 85), but a later and even more masterful stage in his development can be seen on folio 638 recto (page 180). This large miniature must have been painted in the mid-1530s or even a few years later.

When the artists had completed their paintings, they were delivered to the director, who passed them on to the workshop of the illuminators and gilders. Ornamental gilding was the work of specialists, men who, however, were occasionally painters, scribes, poets, or musicians as well. These highly skilled and respected craftsmen were responsible for the richly worked arabesque ornaments that contribute so enormously to the sumptuousness of the book. To these craftsmen also fell the job of ruling, gilding, and coloring the framing rectangles that isolate the text areas, though this humbler task was sometimes assigned to apprentices. Matters of greater moment were the double-page frontispiece with its arabesque and geometric panels, the dedicatory rosette, the chapter headings, and the hundreds of elegantly placed triangles of arabesque that give the text pages much of their sparkling diversity. The illumination of the book, like the illustration, must have gone on over many years. While most of the illuminations were executed after the paintings, there were exceptions to this, as when an artist chose to rearrange a page and the text was written out again to suit his new design.

After the final page had been written, the last miniature painted, and the ultimate bit of illumination completed, the stack of seven hundred and fifty-nine folios was made ready for the binders. Perhaps because of the weight and size of the volume—the pages measure something over twelve by eighteen inches—a particularly sturdy cover was planned rather than the customary delicate one of lacquer. The binding consists of a pair of substantial leather-covered boards, elegantly gilded in two tones of gold and blind-stamped. The inner faces of the boards are adorned with gilding and leather filigree over blue. If it ever existed, the protective outer flap usually found on Iranian books has not survived.

The Artist in Traditional Iran

A GREAT ruler's artists, along with his poets, musicians, philosophers, and other intellectuals, were important court adjuncts, underscoring the patron's might and glory. They were gathered from many sources. At the outset of a dynasty, as when Shah Isma'il founded the Safavid state, the atelier was probably made up mostly of artists and craftsmen taken in the course of political conquest. Ordinarily, however, a prince inherited his painters along with his kingdom. And since artistic talent and training tended to run in families, painting styles were frequently self-perpetuating. At least two sons worked beside their fathers on the Houghton manuscript: Mirza Ali with his father Sultan Muhammad, and Mir Sayyid Ali with Mir Musavvir. Occasionally, in addition, rulers received artists as gifts from well-wishing patrons, while still others were recruited from rival or less consequential workshops or from the artists' guilds that existed in most of the major Iranian painting centers. Membership in the guilds was open to any artist who met the standards. Some artists apparently gained virtually automatic membership through inheritance.

The relationships among the guilds, royal workshops, and market places seem to have been loose. Dust Muhammad, the critic-painter-calligrapher, was hired to work on Bahram Mirza's album, mentioned earlier, on what might be considered a commission basis, despite his position in the workshop of Shah Tahmasp. Another artist, Zayn-al-Abidin, the son of Sultan Muhammad's daughter, is described by Iskandar Munshi as having the patronage of princes, nobles, and grandees, "while his pupils carried on the work of the atelier." Although this took place at a time when, according to Munshi, the royal library had been shut down, it seems to imply that the artist's position ordinarily lay somewhere between full-time royal employment and a commercial career. A *Shah-nameh* dated 1524, now in the Institute for the Peoples of Asia, Leningrad, is pertinent here. On stylistic grounds it can be seen that several of the painters of the Houghton book also worked on this one, but this one is smaller, less fully illustrated, far less rich in appearance, and was probably not a royal commission. At its best, as in its pictures designed and painted by Sultan Muhammad, the Leningrad manuscript is of excellent quality—something that cannot be said of the bulk of Iranian book painting. Like so much of the world's painting, this must be considered goods rather than art. The countless illustrated manuscripts of an uninspired sort turned out by craftsmen of the guilds and commercial workshops for sale to lesser nobles, merchants, and members of religious brotherhoods have given the entire field of Iranian painting, if not a bad name, at least a dull one. Though passably accomplished in technique and finish, these paintings depend as a rule on forms borrowed from the art of the court, and fresh ideas are almost never found in them.

However, the commercial workshops supplied valuable services to both patrons and artists. Great princes not only hired talent from them, they also no doubt released to them artists no longer in favor. If the royal staff was overworked, the princes certainly farmed out jobs to the commercial workshops, either to supply the royal library or to prepare volumes for presentation to distinguished guests, or to be sent to distant friends, or rivals. The artists of the commercial workshops, like those of the court, were expected to present examples of their art to the court upon such occasions as royal births, circumcisions, or special holidays. In exchange, they were given offerings of money, ceremonial robes, or other favors. The bazaars were potential sources of additional income to the royal artists, who might also find greater security working for them than for royalty. The patronage of princes depended upon political good fortune and such variables as continuing enthusiasm or fickle "taste." When princes could no longer afford to support their artists, or when for any reason they refused to do so, the commercial workshops were likely sources of employment. And if no work was available locally, the widespread network of merchants, with their caravans and frequent contacts with other travelers, must have been mines of information as to where artists might find work. News of patronage under the Ottomans, Uzbeks, Mughals, or other Indian sultans must have spread through such channels, which were also responsible for the dissemination of artistic ideas, as when a caravan carried an Iranian mauscript to some remote corner of India.

The painters of a manuscript such as ours can be divided into masters, journeymen, and apprentices or assistants. The masters, at their best men of the stature of Sultan Muhammad, were drawn from varied social milieus. On the uppermost level, many great princes—shahs, khans, sultans, and the like—were themselves more or less gifted amateurs, some of whom subjected themselves to training almost as rigorous as that given the professionals. Concerning the professionals, it should be remembered that in Islam it was possible for people of the humblest birth to attain great position. A gifted, industrious, and fortunate village lad from some remote corner of Fars, for instance, might progress from apprenticeship to a local artisan to a commercial workshop in Shiraz, thence to a governor's library, and finally to eminence in the shah's atelier. Ottoman documents refer to master artists of slave origin. Men of such humble background would have required great wit and charm as well as talent to cut much swath at court; other artists were polished men of the world, born to court circles. The Timurid poet Mir Ali-Shir Nava'i tells us that an artist named Dervish Muhammad was the "milk brother" (sharer of a wet nurse) of a prince. Aqa Mirak, one of the major artists of the Houghton manuscript, was described in contemporary accounts as a "boon companion" of the shah.

Artists' salaries must have varied greatly. A great master and courtier such as Aqa Mirak, or an internationally famed artist such as Bihzad or Sultan Muhammad, probably earned far more than his colleagues. Aqa Mirak, a perfectionist in his use of materials, was given the no doubt lucrative post of *garak yarak,* which made him responsible for the purchasing of all commodities used in the workshops; Bihzad and Sultan Muhammad held the position of chief painter to the court, which must have brought generous payment with it. The Ottoman historian Ali informs us that during the reign of Sultan Sulayman the Magnificent, Shah Quli Naqqash was given a very generous honorarium of one hundred *akçe* upon his arrival at the Ottoman court from Iran. He was also made director of the painting studio attached to the royal court. The financial lot of less august artists is probably suggested by another Ottoman document, and this can be reasonably assumed to reflect Safavid practices as well. It tells us that the daily wage of the most generously paid master among the artists was twenty-four akçes, while the average was about ten, and the lowliest of apprentices, probably a child, received two and a half akçes. These day-to-day rewards were increased by occasional bonuses. An Ottoman document relates that a man earning twenty akçes a day so delighted his patron that he was awarded the great sum of two thousand akçes. Still more generous rewards were probably possible when a prince was feeling wildly indulgent.

Master artists were sometimes differentiated from their apprentices or assistants by being classed as designers or outliners, as opposed to mere painters or colorers or illuminators. However, these explicit terms are not used consistently in the early records. In such a manuscript as ours it is apparent that many of the miniatures were executed wholly by major masters. At other times, lesser masters or assistants painted pictures either entirely alone or with some degree of aid from their betters. Sometimes a master sketched in the design and left its amplification and completion to the assistants. The master's participation varied from a scrawled hint suggesting the disposition of figures or architecture to an elaborate underdrawing requiring little beyond coloring to complete. When an assistant had done his work, a master would sometimes return to add a few improving strokes, or perhaps even a complete figure or two. Additional specialists were occasionally charged with such passages as arabesque ornament on carpets, thrones, or tents. In Mughal India, especially during the reign of Akbar (1557–1605), clerks often wrote the names of the masters (outliners) and assistants (colorers) responsible for a picture in the lower margin; while inscriptions of this sort probably do not occur on manuscripts from Iran, close study of the paintings tells us that the same division of labor was often followed. Since royal Safavid masters played a crucial role in establishing the Mughal school of painting, this is precisely what we might expect.

Whether or not a miniature was wholly by a single master probably concerns us more than it did the Safavid patron or the artist himself. Although individual artists counted for much in Iran's royal workshops (even as their counterparts did in Europe), it was less important whose hand actually executed every square inch of a picture than that it maintained the master's standard. At times we find miniatures designed and largely painted by very distinguished masters, but with parts, such as distant mountain crags or an entire batallion of soldiery, executed by carefully controlled, almost miraculously discreet followers who were only slightly less senior artists themselves. For example, while Sultan Muhammad is responsible for almost all of *The death of Zahhak* (page 117), many of the less important faces in the painting would seem to be the work of the brilliant younger artist Mir Sayyid Ali.

As a rule the more inventive and appealing miniatures are by the major artists working virtually unassisted. The less imaginative or less attractive pictures, which might be likened to houses built by carpenters unaided by architects, are usually by lesser masters or assistants. There are exceptions, of course. Masters at times nodded or were out of sorts, while the lesser men occasionally had moments of high inspiration. For instance, *Sam comes to Mount Alburz* (page 125) is a masterpiece of design and color, and while Sultan Muhammad may have planned it, Painter D is responsible for its every visible stroke.

Technical conventions and visual resources enabled lesser artists to compete on some levels with their betters. Iranian art fed on art more often than on nature, and assistants or apprentices, if called upon to work alone, were likely to resort to art for inspiration. Such painters would generally base their designs on a learned repertoire: upon pictures or parts of pictures available to them either in the workshop or in their patron's library. Most ateliers contained an inherited store of tracings, stencils, pounces, drawings, and miscellaneous scraps—an accumulation of "trade secrets" that may have included motifs derived from exotic sources (Chinese, Indian, European) as well as from earlier phases of the local tradition. If a less inventive or slightly lazy artist wished to paint a picture containing a dragon, he probably found a dragon near at hand to copy. When it was a painted or drawn one, he traced it onto a piece of transparent gazelle skin, then pricked along the outline, thus making a pounce. (At times, too, he simply pricked the original drawing or painting, after placing another sheet of paper beneath it, but this procedure was deemed reprehensible.) He next laid the pounce on the picture in progress and rubbed powdered charcoal through the pinholes. The resulting somewhat rough outline of the dragon would be reinforced with brush and black ink, and corrections might be made in white. Thus far, of course, our painter had accomplished little more than any student could. His ability, or lack thereof, would become evident only as the miniature progressed. A master's pounces were of little avail in the hands of a hack.

While whole compositions were often pounced or traced, and fourteenth-century prototypes are at times recognizable in sixteenth- or seventeenth-century pictures, each generation of artists, however conservative, reinterpreted and altered the ancient designs. Line-for-line copies were rare, and archaistic work was generally restricted to such periods as the late sixteenth and early seventeenth centuries, when patrons were particularly conscious of art history. In our manuscript there are many examples of the continuation of old-fashioned, usually fifteenth-century compositions, but only one series of combats, *The joust of the eleven rooks,* can be considered archaistic. *Fariburz versus Kalbad* (page 165) is one of this series in which the artists—in this case Shaykh Muhammad—deliberately turned back the clock by virtually "quoting" a Herat *Shah-nameh* of about 1440. However, even in this series of paintings the costumes and settings were brought up to date.

Artists of genius, the great masters, soared beyond the barriers of tradition. Although they availed themselves of the storehouses of accumulated motifs, they also invented new ones. Innovators more often opened their eyes to the other source of motifs—nature—which they then interpreted through their own inner visions. The great masters seem to have drawn from life. Instead of tracing someone else's plane tree, crane, or schoolmaster, they left the workshop and took down what they saw with close scrutiny. Their paintings, as a result, are likely to be more convincingly animated than those of less adventurous or less gifted colleagues.

But let us follow the progress of our hypothetical painter, whom we deserted after he had completed the pouncing of a dragon. Like his fellows, he would be seated on the floor, surrounded by his materials, one knee raised to support a wooden or cardboard panel to which his miniature was fastened. To improve his eyesight, perhaps strained by years of close work, he may have worn spectacles, which are known in portraits of Eastern artists at work. Robert Skelton of the Victoria and Albert Museum reports having seen a Mughal portrait of an artist using a magnifying glass, but the use of such cannot have been common. If our painter wanted to paint another dragon next, roaring across the scene from the opposite direction, he had only to turn over his pounce. More likely, however, he required a hero to slay the monster, and he probably found one nearby, ripe for tracing. Dragon by dragon, hero by hero, tree by tree, his composition developed. Needless to say, unless he was gifted, this additive method was likely to result in a poorly coordinated whole. A self-critical and talented artist, while by no means eschewing such time-saving methods, used them with caution as frameworks upon which to improvise. When pounces were used, the composition might be compared to our art of collage, which likewise succeeds or fails through selection and arrangement.

The later stages in the making of a miniature were of necessity less mechanical. The artist was now on his mettle. He had to refine the drawing, choose, perhaps grind and mix the colors, and begin to paint. If he had an individual style it would now become apparent.

Before seeing our painter through the completion of his picture, let us consider some aspects of his technique. Safavid accounts of the art of painting, such as those of Qadi Ahmad or Sadiqi Beg, both of the late sixteenth century, are similar in type to those of medieval Europe. While less detailed than Cennino Cennini's, for example, they are so strikingly parallel in structure that both may go back to common late classical sources. They tell us of very much the same relationships between artists and materials. Although admired and important masters may have had shop assistants to perform sundry technical chores for them, all painters were rigorously trained as children in their craft. Artists became connoisseurs of inks, papers, and other materials. Indeed, some of them were probably so preoccupied with technique and chemistry that they did not spare enough time or energy to paint. Like the Japanese, they cultivated aesthetically "right" ways of treating their supports: suitable methods of cutting, folding, and tearing papers. A skillful paper handler, whose vocation was at times a special craft, knew how to glue sheets together to make cardboard, how to make invisible inlays, and how to marbelize by swirling specially prepared pigments in oil on water and gathering them on paper lifted from below. He could also combine calligraphies, drawings, miniatures, or illuminations with borders in effective ensembles.

Paintbrushes were, of course, very fine, though they can never have consisted of the fabled single hair, which would have made ugly blobs rather than a delicate line. Very personal tools, brushes were usually made by the artist himself to fit his particular grip and needs. Ordinarily, the hairs were plucked from kittens or from the tails of gray squirrels. After painstaking selection, they were tied together and mounted in quills.

Pigments were chosen for brilliance, purity, and—with occasional lapses—permanence. They were composed of many materials, animal, vegetable, and mineral. Since many were costly, both as to raw material and preparation, it is no wonder they were employed with such precision, as though "set" by jewelers whose "gems" were ground lapis lazuli, malachite, vermilion, and gold—to mention but a few. While some pigments were built up in patiently brushed multiple levels, others, such as lapis lazuli and verdigris, could be applied only in single, thick coats. The binding medium was usually glue or size, though gum or egg yolk may also have been employed. A few colors required special binders. In most cases the evenness of tone, brilliance, and permanence suffered if too much or too little medium was used. Verdigris, a corrosive cuprous pigment, could be safely applied only after sealing off the paper with a protective ground. Occasionally the verdigris darkened the surrounding pigments, and at times, despite the protecting seal, it rotted through the paper. Similar preparatory coatings were applied beneath gold and silver. These metallic pigments, acquired from a goldbeater in leaf form, were ground with animal glue and crushed salt in a mortar and afterward kneaded with the fingers. The glue and salt were then washed out of the finely powdered metal.

If gold of a warm hue was desired, a small quantity of copper was added; silver, or perhaps zinc, was added for a lemon tone. After mixture with a special binder (glue size, according to Sadiqi Beg) these metallic paints were brushed on. Frequently they were applied over other colors—for example, when used to decorate costumes—while on other occasions they were themselves ornamented with color or toned with varnishes. For extra glitter, the surface of the gold was often pricked, probably with an ivory stylus or a sharp tooth.

Many pigments were difficult to make. Zinc white required demanding steps involving cookery, smelting, and chemical admixture. Sandarak varnish, for bindings, was not only hard to prepare but dangerous besides. Sadiqi Beg warns that the process should not be attempted near dwelling places. Not only was it a fire hazard; as Qazief points out, it smelled foul.

While most painters of the period we are considering were satisfied with the usual inherited techniques, a few experimented. Sultan Muhammad was not content with flatly applied whites. His turbans, yak-tail whisks, and other appropriate passages were built up in high relief by piling on thick white pigments. This effect was also employed by his followers, as was a device that is occasionally found in earlier miniatures: the use of mother-of-pearl or precious stones, attached for extra richness to rocks, gem-studded ornaments, or leaping fish.

After each area of his picture had been drawn, corrected, gilded or silvered, colored, refined, and further corrected—processes that often must have taken months and in some cases years—our artist's miniature was almost finished. Now, the marginal rulings were completed, and unless the picture was to have a special border of animals, birds, or arabesques, only the burnishing remained. For this, the artist placed the miniature against a hard, smooth surface and rubbed it with a special tool, an agate or possibly a crystal egg. His painting was now ready for inclusion in a manuscript or album.

The Art of Iranian Painting

IRANIAN artists never attempted to hold a mirror to the real world. Instead, they transformed its appearance and spirit into a conventional scheme, the fundamentals of which could probably be traced back to pre-Islamic times. In formal terms, they reduced the solid, three-dimensional world of appearances to an arbitrary two-dimensional scheme. Colors were applied flat, with almost no modeling of either figure or setting. Nonetheless, complicated situations are plausibly represented: battles with great numbers of warriors, horses, and elephants; angels swooping through the heavens; throne scenes crowded with courtiers and attendants. We hardly ever sense that the artist was unduly constrained by his tradition.

Although the two-dimensional convention tended to eliminate trompe l'œil effects—shadows, perspective, modeling, and any strong concern for textural differences (all of which were eventually, by the eighteenth century, adopted through European influence)—the Safavid painter could express almost everything. Recession in space, for example, was implied by overlapping, often in "coulisses," and by placing distant objects toward the top of the picture, nearer ones toward the bottom. At times, distant objects were reduced in size. Gardens, courtyards, and pools—incomprehensible in profile—were rendered as though seen from overhead by a flying bird. Some artists learned to depict people and animals from different points of view, frontally, obliquely, and even with head-on foreshortening; but only miniatures by the most illusionistically oriented painters enable us to "map" precisely where every object, person, or animal stands in relation to the setting.

Admirers of Iranian painting frequently cite its subtlety of color, a quality especially apparent to those who have become used to the darkened, heavily varnished surfaces of pictures painted in the oil medium on canvas. The most creative Iranian artists thought beyond the separate areas of flat hue that they applied so precisely and with such extraordinary concern for crisp outlines. They conceived whole pictures as color compositions, sometimes inventing breathtaking palettes based on relatively simple combinations of two or three colors. Within these schemes they introduced accenting units, small enough to be taken in at a glance—color clusters which lead our eyes from one unit to the next. At times there are as many as a dozen hues of the same color in a single picture, and each such set of variants not only contributes to the design as a whole but can be admired independently, much as the individual voices of a Bach cantata can be enjoyed when heard separately from the whole.

If our artists were concerned with the selection and organization of color, they also employed it for other purposes, such as the establishment of mood. Staccato arrangements of dynamic tones lend clash to battles; a palette of deep red and deep blue simultaneously suggests the emotions of lovers and the darkness of night; and the combination of red, orange, violet, and sulphur yellow sometimes conveys otherworldly awesomeness (page 89).

The representation of even such simple things as night and day was difficult in a tradition that delighted in brilliant, pure color and excluded virtually all illusionism. Artists generally relied on gold or bright blue skies to convey daylight, perhaps with the addition of a glittering rayed sun. Torches, lighted candles, or a moon implied night, though certain artists combined somber colors in palettes suggestive of darkness. Some scenes demanded special effects, such as "snowstorms" of flecked white pigment over entire miniatures.

Color was also employed to inform the observer of specific facts. A green banner or robe implied that its owner was either a Sayyid (descendant of the family of the Prophet) or that he had made the pilgrimage to Mecca. The red upright baton of the Safavid headgear denoted political affiliation. Certain heroes, too, were associated with costumes of a special color or pattern of colors. Rustam's tiger skin, for example, is almost a part of him, while his horse Rakhsh's dappled pinkish-orange hide is tantamount to a uniform. For pictorial purposes, however, artists took liberties with these conventions, as can be seen in the different hues sported by Rakhsh for his many appearances in the Houghton manuscript.

Iranian paintings seldom have single centers of interest. Their compositions do not say, "Look at this hero slaying a dragon!" Rather, they urge us to go beyond the narrative subject to follow rhythms, shapes, and colors sequentially. While some Iranian paintings may strike us forcefully at once, and then—their message conveyed—release us, others invite our eyes to move from one element to the next almost endlessly: from a prince to a princess, pausing for a moment to examine the arabesque on her crown, to a flowering shrub nearby, then onward to a sward of pleasing tufts, a sinuous stream, or a group of convoluted rocks. It is better not to look at all than to hurry.

The varied Iranian line—at times even, wiry, machine-like in its precision, at other times free and spontaneous, or calligraphic—takes its flavor from the close relationship between drawing and fine writing in Islamic countries. The art of calligraphy held a far more prominent place here than in the West. A revulsion in traditional orthodox Islam against the rendering of living things, an act considered to be a pre-emption of God's role as the creator of life, often channeled the visual arts into nonfigurative areas. Writing became one of the major elements in the decoration of architecture, pottery, textiles, jewelry, or almost anything else. Quotations from the Qur'an (Koran) were of course particularly suitable motifs, and these, along with lines of poetry, were inscribed in the many artful scripts that developed over the centuries. Copies of the Qur'an itself were written with enormous care and devotion, both as pious acts on the part of princes and others, and by professional scribes, the best of whom commanded stiff prices for their work. The qualities of fine writing were incorporated by artists, many of whom were also accomplished calligraphers, into figure drawing and painting. The penman's sensitive eye for rhythm, for thicks and thins, and for spacing lent new and singular qualities to the very art which the emphasis on calligraphy had once pushed aside.

Another particularly Islamic development is the ornamental system composed of denaturalized vegetal forms whose reciprocal rhythms so influenced Iranian painting as to make it seem a view of the world in arabesque. This splendid decorative mode, with its live network of curves and countercurves, suffuses many paintings, from entire compositions down to trees, figures, faces, and even curls of hair.

Leaves undulate as if in the wind, cranes flap, warriors hurl javelins—all imbued with life by arabesque rhythms.

Court painting was naturally more literary than the popular art of the bazaars, and, as in its poetry, its images were often metaphorical. This painting's formal elements also recall those of poetry, miniatures and verses alike abounding in subtle tricks of rhythm, ambiguity, and deliberate confusion, perhaps to heighten by contrast our appreciation of their technical perfection. Court painters occasionally teased with seeming lapses—an effect like that of a juggler feigning clumsiness. An amusing and common hyperbole is the depiction of an animal's head emerging from behind a rock too small to conceal its body.

Although particularly gifted and inspired artists devised new and psychologically convincing characters, many of the players in the Houghton manuscript are portrayed conventionally, their gestures conforming to ancient traditions. The frequent finger to mouth, urging silence in our culture, conveys astonishment in theirs; a man holding his hands upon his ears is signifying deepest respect, not sensitivity to noise. To the Safavid, many of the players' appearances must have evoked semiautomatic responses, like ours at a Punch and Judy show. Most of their characterizations are universal and easily understood: the cypress-like young hero and his rose-vine of a heroine (occasionally represented metaphorically as a cypress entwined by flowering vines), both with faces like full moons; the girl's wise old nurse, whose nannyish caution blends with true devotion; the venerable sage, grizzled in beard, reserved in manner; the swashbuckling heavy-set paladin or knight, accompanied by his discreet young page; and the reliable peasant or herdsman, smelling of the stable and honest to the core. No less important are the lions, demons, witches, and monsters whose antics and infamies keep the human performers on their mettle, and whose blood spatters so decoratively across many of the miniatures in our manuscript. If these stock types appear familiar or trite to us, how much more so they must have seemed to the Safavids! Yet in sixteenth-century Iran they were certainly relished, just as we relish our own cadre of villainous saloonkeepers, gun-toting cowpokes, and innocent maidens. However, the Safavids' devotion to types, like ours, seldom restrained them from also ridiculing them.

In Iranian painting, and notably in the Houghton manuscript, we must be prepared for burlesque as well as the sublime. Mock heroism is evident in bold Faridun's wandering eye, which fastens on a girl in an upper window even as he smites the wicked Zahhak (page 113). And what could be ruder or funnier than the glimpses we are given into military life when potulent veterans are attacked after a night of carousing (page 156)?

An unusual and appealing characteristic of the Houghton manuscript is its range of humor, from that of the earthy mood of early Safavid art (when the atmosphere of Shah Isma'il's armed camps yet prevailed) to the refinement and elegance of Shah Tahmasp's court in the late 1530s or early 40s. In the later miniatures wit is more in evidence than broad comedy. Repartee evokes snickers rather than guffaws, and much of our amusement results from the artists' penetrating observation of human quirks. In the earlier pictures, which are usually more popular in nature, we encounter Rabelaisian situations, depending less upon the precise analysis of mental states than upon bodily appearances or gestures. But we are rarely shocked by Iranian miniatures, perhaps because they all stem from the more genteel or formal strata of society. (Most of the exceptions appear to have been made for patrons with penchants for the "curious.") At particularly refined courts (notably those of the late fourteenth-century Jalayirids, Sultan Husayn Mirza's Herat, or Shah Tahmasp's circle in the 1540s), potentially offensive subjects were rendered innocuous by complex elaboration: lovers *in flagrante delicto* were painted small and draped; blood was shed in decorative patterns, more evocative of a champagne fountain than the battlefield.

Too often Iranian painting is thought to be an ultrasophisticated, hedonistic art. In fact, it is an integral part of the many-faceted civilization from which it emerged. There is, to be sure, decorative art to soothe and please, erotic art to excite, and satiric art to entertain, but although intended to delight and amuse its young patron, a book such as the *Shah-nameh* was meant simultaneously to instruct. Its tales summarize the lore of the civilization in which it was created. At once a history, political text, and religious treatise, it is a compendium of the body and mind, the intuition and intellect, of an entire culture. Its illustrations, in addition, give us reliable insights into the appearance and manners of Shah Tahmasp's court.

The religious elements in Iranian painting are generally little understood in the West, perhaps mainly because of the difference in traditions of religious subject matter in the Muslim and Christian worlds. In the West, until recently, religious institutions were among the major sources of patronage, and an art illustrative of our religion's myths—crucifixions, annunciations, likenesses of prophets and saints—was suited to church, palace, and home alike. In Islam, religious art of this sort is rare. The Qur'an was not illustrated, and mosque walls were not adorned with pictures, sacred or otherwise. The fact that Islam did not often provide opportunities for religious representations does not mean, however, that religious art did not exist. Books on theology, lives of saints, and texts about such matters as the pilgrimage to Mecca were illustrated. On rare occasions, as in our culture also, such illustrations are religious in feeling as well as subject. At times, too, a poet such as Nizami describes religious episodes; for example, the ascent of the Prophet, a subject that seems to have inspired some few truly religious works of art. Ultimately, however, deeply religious painting, in Islam as in the West, depends on a mystical or pantheistic quality, not on a specific iconography. When an individual artist is of a religious temperament, he is likely to produce religious pictures. Sultan Muhammad's *Court of Gayumars* is outwardly concerned with the story of Iran's first ruler, but even a glance at it confirms that there is far more beneath. The mountainside teems with visionary beings from the spirit world, perhaps souls awaiting rebirth. This picture must be recognized as one of the world's great mystical works of art.

Two Traditions: Painting at Herat and Tabriz

THE Houghton *Shah-nameh* and Safavid painting in general synthesize two major strands in what might be termed the Turko-Iranian tradition. One of these is the school of the Timurid dynasty as represented at the court of Sultan Husayn Mirza of Herat, in the eastern region; the other is that of Tabriz, in northwestern Iran, which had been the capital of the Aq-Qoyunlu Turkmans. Among the cities that fell to Shah Isma'il when he conquered Iran in the early sixteenth century, these two contained the most dynamic and creative ateliers of painting.

If in the late fifteenth century we had met princes of the Timurid and Turkman houses, it would have been difficult to differentiate between these rivals, for they shared a common culture. Their languages were the same, they read the same poets, and they vied with one another to hire the same intellectuals, musicians, and other notables. Yet there were differences between them, and these differences are reflected in their paintings, which could be likened to pictures from Siena and Florence, where local variations upon the same themes and in the name of the same God are unmistakable. Timurid painting is well known to us today from the studies of Ivan Stchoukine and others (though its earliest phases await further investigations in the albums and manuscripts of the Topkapu Seray Museum). Turkman painting, in contrast, has not yet been defined. For one thing, inscribed Turkman material has not yet been adequately published, so the style is still the subject of much speculation. No doubt the Istanbul libraries will in time reveal enough dated examples of Tabriz painting for one to trace fully the development of the school. Meanwhile, it is possible to suggest very broadly some characteristics of the style, and to illustrate a few examples that shed light upon the Turkman contributions to the Houghton *Shah-nameh.*

First, let us look briefly at the better-known Timurid style—not tracing its history but rather examining one work by its supreme genius, Bihzad. The marvelous *Bustan* manuscript of Sa'di made in Herat in 1488/89 for the last great Timurid prince, Sultan Husayn Mirza (1468–1506), in no sense reflects the development of Timurid painting as a whole, yet it is in many ways the perfect embodiment of Timurid characteristics on the highest level of the court idiom. Sultan Husayn's particular areas of expression were neither politics nor soldiering (though in his youth he had shown himself a bold, strong, and wise warrior). Although he was an inheritor of might, his own greatest prowess lay elsewhere: in his capacities as poet and creative patron. This philosopher-king surrounded himself with brilliant intellectuals: poets such as Mir Ali-Shir Nava'i and artists of whom the most renowned was Bihzad.

At the time of the 1488 *Bustan* Bihzad was clearly at the height of his powers, temperamentally fulfilled, and thus ideally matched to his inspired patron. In partnership, they produced several of the world's outstanding manuscripts. Under wise, stimulating patronage, Bihzad's talent had reached a confrontation with the world of reality. He opened his eyes to nature and transformed what he saw into a vision that is restrained, technically perfect, supremely realistic, and yet all-encompassing. His sensitive observation bore fruit in the unprecedented naturalism of the *Bustan*'s five miniatures. In one of these (FIGURE 1), a sprightly treatise on liquor, an Indian couple at the upper right operate an elegant still, while the husband sings to his wife, accompanying himself on a vina. Below, portrait-like servants decant spirits into a miscellany of jugs and bottles rendered with a still-life painter's attention to shapes, colors, and textures. Another acute glimpse of everyday life from this manuscript depicts an old man washing between his toes, attended by a black servant offering a slightly mussed towel. But while Bihzad's searching interest in the world about him was a fresh departure, he adapted what he saw to the prevailing idiom. Although he was a passionate observer of human foibles, his tottering drunks, peasants, and beggars are never vulgar or ill-mannered. His characterizations are always tolerant, even loving, and his wit is at all times in perfect tone. Even when he was absorbed in technical innovation, and built up pigments to suggest rough textures so thickly that they have cracked and flaked, he never weakened his poetic vision by virtuosity. Such a miniature as *Yusuf fleeing from Zulayka,* in the Cairo *Bustan,* is made all the more moving by the tautly logical handling of space in the claustrophobic palace—all closed doors and staircases—from which the hero is striving to escape. In Bihzad's pictures one knows precisely where every character stands in space, what he is doing, and what he is thinking. But though the settings with their exquisite arabesques are elaborate, the colors rich, the costumes detailed, the characterizations of people and animals psychologically penetrating, none of these elements outweighs the others. In these miniatures Bihzad's work is always harmoniously balanced—mind and body, intellect and intuition, are fully integrated.

Let us now turn to the Turkman style. Its character on a courtly level can be studied in a copy of Nizami's *Khamseh,* written at Tabriz in 1481 by Abd al Rahim al Ya'qubi, one of the royal scribes in the employ of Ya'qub Beg, the Turkman

FIGURE 1 *The distillation, consumption, and effects of liquor,* by Bihzad, from a *Bustan* of Sa'di dated 1488/89.

Egyptian National Library, Cairo

FIGURE 2 *Bahram Gur in the yellow pavilion,* from a *Khamseh* of Nizami written in 1481 at Tabriz.

Topkapu Seray Museum Library, Istanbul, H. 762

sultan. The manuscript, now in the Topkapu Seray Museum Library, was begun for the sultan's brother, Pir Budak, continued for another brother, Khalil, and only then worked on for the sultan—and it remained unfinished. It contains nineteen miniatures, of which nine, two incomplete, were painted in the late fifteenth century. The other ten were completed or wholly painted for Shah Isma'il after he captured Tabriz (1501). One of the earlier miniatures, *Bahram Gur in the yellow pavilion* (FIGURE 2), is perhaps intended as a portrait of Sultan Ya'qub himself. In the pavilion the prince reclines languorously on cushions attended by a princess; outside, in a flowery landscape, the same prince peeps amorously at the same princess, seated beside a stream. In spite of its finish and refinement, this miniature is imbued with a dynamic verve that differentiates it from the more controlled style of Bihzad. In some respects it seems less developed than the almost contemporary miniatures of the Herat master. There is little of Bihzad's psychological penetration, little of his correctness of proportion, and even less of his logical handling of space. Instead, the Turkman artist delights us with his fantasy world, which catches us up in its brighter hues (rich lapis lazuli, salmon pink, orange, and a multitude of bright accents set against tan, pale green, and pale blue-violet grounds). His world is composed of dragon-claw clouds, cliffs containing a wondrous hidden zoo of amiable beasts and monsters, stones and rocks that belong in a jeweler's window, and highly stylized, Chinese-influenced flowers. These last are particularly characteristic of Turkman art, virtual earmarks of the idiom. They lend the entire picture the sweetness of a spring bouquet, yet they are in most cases derived from art rather than directly from nature. Forms in them whirl and spin, or soar and plunge, like pinwheels and skyrockets. Often too large, they seem to have burgeoned from a tropical jungle. If we look closely at this picture, there are surprises. A rabbit in the foreground emerges from a hole to feed on wispy grass, ducks peer at one another on the silver stream, game birds look on from the pinnacles. Few pictures could better describe heaven on earth.

But what else makes this picture Turkman rather than Timurid? Its slightly archaic flavor? Its almost excessive vitality? Its greater urgency and intensity of color? Or all of these things and still other, lesser details?—the cushions and robes with their vigorous designs of orientalizing dragons and birds; the taste for strong spots, stripes, and other ornamental patterns; the figure drawing, with its expressive rather than naturalistic proportions; the effective but spatially illogical treatment of architecture and setting; the concealed grotesques in the landscape. In combination, these are elements of a unique style, one of the most compelling in all Islamic art. Turkman painting reminds us of certain schools of Indian painting, as at Ahmednagar, Bijapur, and Golconda in the Deccan. The spirit is more Dionysian than Apollonian. Tensions are less resolved here than in Timurid painting; Turkman miniatures fairly soar from the page. In gastronomic terms, we enjoy a particularly rich paté de foie gras shot through with a superabundance of truffles. Excess!

To understand further the character of the Turkman idiom, let us turn to an album that has been in Istanbul for generations—Topkapu Seray Library H. 2153. Although it is not certain when this huge volume, often called in Turkey the Album of the Conqueror, reached the Ottoman court, it may well have been captured during one of the Ottoman invasions of Tabriz in the early sixteenth century. On the other hand, it may have been presented to the Ottomans by the

FIGURE 3 *Sultan Ya'qub Beg(?) and his court,* Tabriz, about 1480.
Topkapu Seray Museum Library H. 2153

Safavids, who probably acquired it when they took Tabriz in 1501. The volume was probably formed by Ya'qub Beg, the Turkman sultan; his name is traditionally associated with it. Now bound in nineteenth-century red morocco, it is a grandiose scrapbook, containing calligraphies (many of them by Ya'qub's scribes, and none, so far as we know, later than his reign); European prints, including fifteenth-century Italian engravings; rather inferior bazaar paintings from China; local copies and variants of these; and an assortment of Mongol, Jalayirid, and Timurid paintings—in sum, just the sort of material that would have been collected by the Turkmans. Most of the album, however, is composed of magnificent miniatures and drawings made for the Turkmans by their own artists.

A group portrait in the album can be assumed to depict Sultan Ya'qub himself, along with his noble assembly, glowering with animal energy beneath a stunning blue and white canopy (FIGURE 3). Costumes, faces—slightly doll-like but with lively side glances—proportions, and colors are precisely those found in the Tabriz *Khamseh* of 1481. In fact the *Khamseh* miniature, *Bahram Gur in the yellow pavilion,* was probably painted by the same artist. Most characteristic is the vegetation that forms a dynamic tapestry beneath and behind the assembly. Such flowers, trees, and foliage are among the most telling marks of the Turkman idiom, accounting for its pulsating lushness. Although Timurid and Turkman painting alike abound in backgrounds composed of clumps and flowers and grasses, in the latter they are wilder and more frankly Chinese in derivation. Long yellow-outlined petals bend and twist, outsize peony blossoms and palmettes seem to expand on the page, and tremblingly sensitive fronds, breaking downward, glut our eyes with their powerful interrelated forms. Such exoticism was to be expected at Tabriz, long the major center in Iran of trade between East and West. Textiles, pottery, metalwork, and paintings were brought here from China as well as from India and Europe by caravans of merchants. It would be astonishing indeed if exotic motifs had not influenced local artists and patrons. Trade, however, was not the sole reason for the impact of oriental ideas. During the fourteenth century Tabriz had been in Mongol hands, and the Mongols had an inbred taste for Chinese imports.

Dragons were a favorite element in Tabriz art, and a dragon scene from a great Mongol *Shah-nameh* of the mid-fourteenth century represents a vital early stage of this school that continued to flower until its qualities merged with those of the Timurid style in the early years of the Houghton manuscript. The painting (FIGURE 4) is as compelling as any we know in Turko-Iranian art. The action arrests us by having been drawn to the very front of the picture plane. The hero, Bahram Gur, his back to us, confronts the expiring monster, thrusting into his vitals a mighty sword, exerting with a fierce gesture every measure of his strength. The vast, hulking form is drawn in an even, powerful line that undulates across the page, coiling like some great snake round the trunk of an ornamentally Chinese tree. While this appears to shrivel under the pressure of the monster's last effort, the dragon's once menacing paws flop in the air like a kitten's. In contrast to the monster, Bahram Gur's horse gazes calmly upon the lurid spectacle, as if stench and guts were all in a day's work. Beyond and above the dying dragon's maw, a zigzag of sharply defined rocks, bristling with a rasp of vegetation, con-

FIGURE 4
Bahram Gur slaying a dragon, from the Demotte *Shah-nameh,* Tabriz, mid-14th century.

The Cleveland Museum of Art, Purchase, Grace Rainey Rogers Fund

FIGURE 5
Demons with a dragon, Tabriz, about 1485.

Topkapu Seray Museum Library H. 2153

tributes to the cruel atmosphere and draws our attention by its stabbing angles to all the horrors accompanying the monster's end. His dying sounds fairly rattle from the page.

Although we cannot further explore here the development of Tabriz painting during the period of the Turkman dynasties, we must meet at least one late fifteenth-century dragon as well as a pair of *divs,* or demons, essential members of the Turkman painted cast of characters. A drawing from the great Istanbul album brings such a group together (FIGURE 5), along with a clump of characteristic vegetation to establish the connection between such drawings and the *Khamseh* of 1481. In this instance the dragon and the divs are unusually tame. One often

FIGURE 6
Lions in a landscape,
Tabriz, about 1480.

Topkapu Seray Museum Library H. 2153

encounters less amiable creatures in Turkman drawings and miniatures. Some are nightmarishly horrible, as in a painting of hairy divs who have torn a white stallion into bite-size chunks.

Let us end this attempt at characterizing Aq-Qoyunlu Turkman art by looking at a marvelous miniature of two lions in the same Istanbul album (FIGURE 6). These benevolently smiling beasts beneath a very Chinese blossoming tree would seem to be of about the same date as the album's group portrait. Here, the outburst of ornamental flowers, a side issue in the group portrait, is the key to the curvilinear character of the whole, which radiates all that is happiest in the animal, vegetable, and mineral kingdoms. Concealed spirits in the rocks smile at us, birds chatter, and even butterflies seem bent upon celebration. No wonder that Sultan Muhammad was inspired by this Turkman miniature when he painted a pair of comparable lions beneath the rustic throne of Gayumars in the Houghton book, a picture that might be considered the climax of the Tabriz idiom under the Turkmans even though it was painted in the Safavid period.

Painting during the Reigns of Shah Isma'il and Shah Tahmasp

THE Houghton manuscript records the development of an art style, and of an Iranian dynasty, with the exactitude of a logbook. Through its pages it is possible to trace the development of the Safavid ethos as represented by its artists and patrons. The creation of the volume can be likened to an epic in itself, with a lengthy and complex plot and a cast of hundreds. Here we can consider only the major players: the first two Safavid rulers, a few of their artists, and one or two of their courtiers.

Shah Isma'il was descended from the Sufi shaykh of Ardabil, in Azerbaijan, Safi al-Din, who died in 1334 after forming a dervish order, the Safaviyeh. Although the Safavids spoke Turkish, they were probably of Kurdish origin, and Shaykh Safi al-Din himself was probably a member of the Sunni sect of Muslims. His successors, however, became militant and extremist members of the Shi'ite sect, which gained many converts among the Turkman tribes of Azerbaijan, Iraq, Anatolia, and Syria. In the mid-fifteenth century, on the death of the grandson of the founder, the sect split into a conservative wing and an extremist wing. The conservatives remained peacefully in Ardabil; the extremists moved into Anatolia and Syria, where the order developed an increasingly military character. At first the Safavids were protected by Uzun Hasan, the Aq-Qoyunlu Turkman leader, but after Uzun Hasan's death in 1478 the military nature of the Safavid extremists was disturbingly clear. In a clash between Ya'qub Beg, the successor to the Aq-Qoyunlu leadership, and Haydar, the Safavid leader, Haydar was killed. His sons, Sultan Ali, Ibrahim, and the infant who would become Shah Isma'il, were imprisoned in the castle of Istakhr, in the southern province of Fars. Later, during the reign of Rustam Aq-Qoyunlu, 1492–97, the Safavid princes, his cousins, were released to lead their dervish army against Rustam's enemies. In the next development, Rustam turned against Sultan Ali, and the Safavid was killed in battle against the Aq-Qoyunlu. The child Isma'il fled to the Caspian province of Gilan, hid there until 1499, and then, at the age of twelve, made his bid for power. In Anatolia he was joined by many converts, including whole tribes, who became the basis of the Safavid army, the Qizil Bash ("Redheads"), named for their distinctive headdress of turban wound round a scarlet upright.

In 1500 Isma'il defeated and killed Farrukh-Yasar, the Safavids' traditional enemy within the Aq-Qoyunlu Turkman family. A year later Isma'il defeated Alvand, the co-ruler of the Aq-Qoyunlu. Shortly thereafter he occupied Tabriz and crowned himself shah, after which he proclaimed Shi'ism the state religion. In 1503 he captured Shiraz, crushing Murad, the ruler of the southern and western portions of the once vast Aq-Qoyunlu empire. He then turned to the east and in 1510, at Merv, defeated and slew Shaybani Khan, the Uzbek leader who had taken Herat from the Timurids on the death of Sultan Husayn Mirza in 1506. Herat and the entire region of Khorasan now came under Isma'il's control.

Shah Isma'il's intensity can yet be felt. This red-headed strong man, "amiable as a girl but more powerful than any of his courtiers," according to a contemporary traveler, brings to mind another conqueror, Babur, who also combined military prowess, buoyant optimism, guilt-free ruthlessness, and a love of literature, art, and music. When he was not on campaign, Shah Isma'il lived in the Aq-Qoyunlu palace in Tabriz, and here he virtually retired after 1514. According to a Venetian who visited Tabriz in 1518, "This Sophy [Sufi] is loved and reverenced by his people as a god, and especially by his soldiers, many of whom enter into battle without armor, expecting their master, Isma'il, to watch over them in the fight." Isma'il was charismatic. More than this, he was a poet and a visionary. In his ecstatic poetry he called himself God. He wrote raw heresy: "I am Faridun, Khosrow, Iskandar, Jesus, Zahhak." "I am the staff of Moses." "The signs of Noah have appeared in me; the Flood is bursting forth." Whether or not we take his poems as deliberate appeals to his extremist soldiers (many of them were written during the years of warfare), they represent an important aspect of the shah's character and reflect the spirit of the early Safavid court.

Shah Isma'il's visionary poems are similar in spirit to the earliest Safavid paintings we know: those that illustrate a copy of Asafi's *Dastan-i Jamal u Jalal* in the library of Uppsala University. A very clear colophon dated 1502/03 names Herat as this manuscript's place of origin and the scribe as Sultan Ali, whom we assume to be Sultan Ali Qayini rather than his more renowned namesake, Sultan Ali al-Mashhadi. Sultan Ali Qayini is known from other manuscripts written at Herat. Two of the *Jamal u Jalal* miniatures are dated, one inscribed with the equivalent of 1503/04, the other 1504/05.

Why should Herat, the Timurid capital, be the source of this earliest dated manuscript containing Safavid miniatures? The first painting in the volume, while stylistically like most of the others, shows figures who do not wear the Safavid baton turban. Presumably it was painted in Herat for a local patron. The rest of the pictures, most of which show figures with Safavid headgear very unlikely to have been depicted in Herat work, were probably added in Safavid territory, to which the uncompleted manuscript must have gone. This explanation is plausible if we consider the political situation at Herat during the period. There were yearly civil wars in which the sons of Sultan Husayn Mirza, the ruler of the Timurid state, were pitted against their father. One of them in fact cooperated with the Safavids and joined with Shah Isma'il when he campaigned in Mazandaran in 1504. The *Jamal u Jalal* was presumably brought to Isma'il in incomplete form at this time, along with its artist or artists who then joined the gathering Safavid ateliers.

Stylistically, these early Safavid paintings (FIGURE 7) are quite unlike those of Sultan Husayn's Timurid workshop as directed by Bihzad. Far less detailed, and containing round-faced figures, flattened architecture and landscapes, and turbulent orientalized clouds and vegetation, the *Jamal u Jalal* pictures represent an urbanized version of the style to be found in an earlier manuscript, a *Khavaran-nameh* of Ibn Husam, the text and many miniatures of which are now in the Museum of Decorative Arts, Teheran. The Iranian scholar Yaha Zuka has proposed that the pictures of this epic, telling of the wars and exploits of holy Ali, sacred to the Shi'ah sect, were painted for a cloister of the Mevlevi order, an attribution that is consistent with the manuscript's occasional flashes of religious fervor. Morover, Zuka has pointed out that these so-called dancing dervishes had important centers near Konya and in northern Khorasan, but none whatsoever in the south. He ascribes the *Khavaran-nameh* to the area of Herat, which is consistent with its close stylistic affinities to the *Jamal u Jalal.* Although the *Khavaran-nameh* contains the date 1477, its many miniatures are likely to have been painted over a period of a decade or longer. One of its most visionary pages (FIGURE 8) would seem to be an earlier work by the same master who painted most of the *Jamal u Jalal,* including the page we reproduce. As such, it exemplifies another important strand in the formation of the new synthesis of Safavid art, which—as one might suppose—emerged from the many centers of painting brought together by Shah Isma'il's conquests.

We have already discussed the magnificent *Khamseh* begun for the Aq-Qoyunlu royal family in Tabriz in 1481, noting the relationship of its delightful miniatures to pictures in the Istanbul Album of the Conqueror. With his capture of Tabriz, Shah Isma'il came into possession of this *Khamseh* along with the rest of the royal library. Its unfinished miniatures were now completed by the shah's young atelier, directed, it would seem, by the artist who had led the work on the *Jamal u Jalal.* For instance, *Bahram Gur in the white pavilion* (FIGURE 9) combines stylistic elements from the *Jamal u Jalal* and from the Aq-Qoyunlu paintings made for the *Khamseh* during the first period of its creation. Here and elsewhere in the late miniatures we find the doll-like faces, the expressive rather than naturalistic proportions, the bold scale, and the fervor of the Herat *Khavaran-nameh* intermixed with the more sophisticated elements of the highest level of the Tabriz school under the Aq-Qoyunlu Turkmans.

FIGURE 7 *Jamal before the turquoise dome,* from a *Dastan-i Jamal u Jalal* dated 1502/03. The painting is dated (inscription above door) 1504/05.

Uppsala University Library, Uppsala, Sweden

FIGURE 8 *Gabriel announcing the apotheosis of Ali,* by Sultan Muhammad, from a *Khavaran-nameh* dated 1477.

Private collection

FIGURE 9 *Bahram Gur in the white pavilion,* by Sultan Muhammad, early 16th century, from the 1481 *Khamseh* of Nizami. See caption to figure 2.

FIGURE 10 *Sleeping Rustam,* by Sultan Muhammad, early 16th century.

British Museum 1948-12-11-023. Copyright British Museum

The culmination of this idiom is evident in an unfinished *Shah-nameh* miniature in the British Museum, *Sleeping Rustam* (FIGURE 10). This painting is the direct equivalent of the visionary side of Shah Isma'il's personality, the aspect also represented by his ecstatic poetry. It can also be seen as the high point in the early development of his leading artist, Sultan Muhammad, who must have been the head of the workshop that illustrated the *Jamal u Jalal* and added to the *Khamseh* after this Turkman manuscript fell into Shah Isma'il's hands. An earlier phase in the development of this artist can be seen in the *Khavaran-nameh* miniature. The style, which was slightly raw and awkward in the picture of Gabriel, is masterful in the *Sleeping Rustam,* but in both the artist's personality shines forth. Above all, he is bent on expressiveness. He is little concerned with real space, as evidenced by his relationship of the landscape to the animals or the seeming flying carpet upon which Rustam naps. Instead, he wishes to move us with the wonder of the story and stun us with the enchantment of the setting. The power of the *Sleeping Rustam* is intense, like an explosion contained. There is hardly a point of rest anywhere. Each leaf or tendril, each bending tree trunk or flame-like rush vibrates with a turbulent rhythm. Rich, fresh color—a tropical forest of greens, reddish brown, ginger, pink, red, violet, and more—and an almost incredibly dense texture raise the mood to ecstatic pitch, fulfilling the promise of the *Khavaran-nameh* page. While the earlier painting is rewarding to explore, especially the vibrant forms of its tapestry-like greenery, this one catches us up in all its parts. The tale is most affectionately recounted. We are urged to stroll through the lush undergrowth. In doing so we encounter a giant snake, gloating like a satisfied dragon as it gulps down a tiny bird. Looking closer still, we are startled by the strident protests of a pair of luckier warblers. And if our eyes move a little upward and to the right, we meet a smiling tiger-spirit concealed in a rock, seemingly vicariously delighted by the snake's meal, much as a huntsman's ghost might enjoy watching the triumph of a latter-day hunter. Note, too, the witty characterization of the sleeping hero, irritable at having his rest interrupted. And the hero's steed: only a very great master could have painted this fiery-eyed Rakhsh, with his electrically charged mane, and only a draughtsman of total authority could have made us feel the crunch of the lion's jaw on Rakhsh's fetlock.

Although the *Sleeping Rustam* was probably in the most representative style at the court of Shah Isma'il, to whose nature it was so well suited, there may also have been a Tabriz version of the Bihzadian idiom of Herat. A *Divan* of Hafiz, dated 1512, in the Walters Art Gallery, Baltimore, is a likely example. Such a

strand of painting as it shows would be perfectly in keeping with Shah Isma'il's draw to orthodoxy, which led him to forge documents in 1508 (the year of some of his most heretical verse) to prove his descent from the Sayyids (the family of the Prophet), a bold deception which included a false genealogical tree.

Let us now consider the impact of Bihzad upon the art of Tabriz. This was first felt strongly in 1522, when young Prince Tahmasp, eventually the patron of the Houghton manuscript, returned from Herat. In 1516, when he was less than two, he had been sent by his father to Herat as governor. However odd or even cruel it may seem to us to uproot a child from his family, this was not at the time an unusual procedure. Infant princes were likely to be sent abroad in the charge of a *lala,* who combined the responsibilities of regent, tutor, and father. This custom explains the lack of loving family relationships in the uppermost ranks of the Turko-Iranian world, where brothers unfamiliar with one another and sons hardly knowing their fathers often engaged in gory struggles for power. In this instance, it also altered the nature of Iranian painting.

Herat had been the capital of Sultan Husayn Mirza, the last and possibly greatest of the Timurid patrons. Many of the intellectuals, musicians, artists, and artisans who had contributed to the flowering of his court were still present when Prince Tahmasp arrived. Growing up in Herat was for a Safavid prince like being sent to Athens for a young Roman. In this case, however, the infant's departure from Tabriz was probably first ascribable to the political need to station a member of the royal family near the Uzbek frontier, and second to his father's admiration for the culture of the Timurid center.

During his years at Herat the prince was no doubt exposed to daily encounters with wise graybeards: learned doctors to expound on the Qur'an and its laws, artful calligraphers, witty and occasionally profound poets, masters of proper conduct and manners who had contributed to the graces of the Timurid court and would now pass on their niceties of protocol to the Safavid fledgling, mathematicians spinning webs of intricate abstraction, historians who could expound the wisdom or follies of previous khans, sultans, and shahs. And these were but a few of our prince's mentors. By torchlight, or while seated in a tree house or by a garden brook, he must have heard recitations from the poetical classics, perhaps read from noble copies prepared for his own library. To train his body, a succession of grizzled veterans put the boy through a course of horseback riding as soon as he could be placed on a saddle. Archery, sword practice, and polo would have been added at the earliest possible moment. And of course there were lessons in painting and connoisseurship, and these very probably brought him in touch with Sultan Husayn's greatest artist, Bihzad.

Bihzad's career after the fall of Herat to the Uzbeks in 1507 is shadowy. According to the Ottoman historian Ali, Shah Isma'il had expressed anxiety over his fate at the battle of Chaldiran in 1514, but this account, which includes a problematic reference to the calligrapher Shah Mahmud Nishapuri, is probably fictitious. It is likely that Bihzad remained in Herat until he went to Tabriz with Prince Tahmasp when the boy was recalled after a political crisis in Herat. Bihzad was appointed director of the royal library by Shah Isma'il on April 24, 1522. Had he been in Tabriz earlier, he would surely have received this appointment sooner, and his direct influence on Tabriz painting would have been felt prior to the prince's return.

Whenever he reached Tabriz, it is certain that the Timurid old master was no longer in his prime. Surviving examples of his later work, such as a roundel in the Freer Gallery of Art showing an old man and a boy in a landscape, lack the fineness of touch of his earlier work. Even so, the roundel composition, an original one in Islamic art, is brilliantly inventive. While Qadi Ahmad writes that Bihzad illustrated a *Khamseh* copied for Shah Tahmasp in minute script by Shah Mahmud Nishapuri, his most active role in Tabriz, where he died in 1536, was probably that of mentor rather than practitioner.

This is demonstrated by a fascinating pocket-size copy of Arifi's *Guy u Chawgan (The Ball and the Polo Stick),* dated 1523/24, now in Leningrad, which was presented by its scribe to Qadi-yi Jahan. The precocious ten-year-old scribe was Prince Tahmasp himself, and the book was written just prior to his father's death during his return from a pilgrimage to Ardabil. The recipient was Prince Tahmasp's recently reassigned lala, who had been with him during the early years at Herat and would continue to be a major figure in his life until 1550.

The importance of the little *Guy u Chawgan* in the development of Safavid painting would be hard to overemphasize. The style of its miniatures tells us precisely what was then admired in the most august circles of the future shah's court. That style was Bihzad's, whose minutely detailed figures and and poetically naturalistic landscapes, often edged with little scraggly trees and stumps, are found throughout. Neatly, if not superbly, written and richly illuminated, the book contains sixteen contemporary unsigned miniatures, most of which can be attributed on stylistic grounds to the leading court artists. The first of them, a double-page outdoor throne scene, seems to have been painted by Bihzad himself, whose eyesight must have further failed after he painted the Freer roundel. Perhaps he was assisted by Dust Muhammad, the artist-calligrapher-historian, who was probably also in Prince Tahmasp's Herat retinue. The other miniatures are so markedly Bihzadian that one can only suppose the old Herat artist closely supervised them or perhaps in a few instances supplied outlines for them. Even such a longtime Safavid luminary as Sultan Muhammad, contributing several miniatures to the project (FIGURE 11), adjusted his style so well to Bihzad's that only hints of his earlier and later idioms are recognizable.

In the *Guy u Chawgan* we find the moment of confrontation between the Herat mode of Bihzad and the Tabriz style of Sultan Muhammad—in turn a development of the Aq-Qoyunlu court style—and the manner of the 1502/03 *Jamal u Jalal,* which had emerged from the style we noted in the *Khavaran-nameh.* The prince's artists were emulating the style of Bihzad in the *Guy u Chawgan.* They were wearing his garb, but the mantle did not quite fit as yet

FIGURE 11
A polo match, by Sultan Muhammad, from a *Guy u Chawgan* of Arifi dated 1523/24.

Leningrad Public Library D.N. CDXLI

and the shoes pinched. There are few signs here of the forthcoming fusion between the visionary manner of Shah Isma'il's leading artists and the manner so recently imported in its purest form from Herat.

It is of course not surprising that this book copied by the prince should so strongly mirror the spirit of Herat's most eminent artist. Conceivably, however, the taste of its miniatures also reflects the penchants of Qadi-yi Jahan, who was powerfully influential during the prince's formative years. As a boy and adolescent, Tahmasp probably took great comfort, even refuge, in art, for the period of his regency, during which he was seldom in Tabriz, was a time of trial. Civil wars, family squabbles, invasions by the Ottomans and Uzbeks, desertions, and almost constant military campaigns combined to make his young life anything but easy, especially if we consider the psychological wounds that must have come from his uprooting as an infant. According to Sam Mirza, his brother, Tahmasp caused wondering comment when he spent many hours mysteriously occupied at a house in the environs of Tabriz. These mysterious rendezvous were probably with his painters.

Although his intense enthusiasm for art must have developed at Herat, it may not have been known to his father until the boy's return in 1522. When the estranged, probably very cowed, son met his dynamic, conquering father again (or, really, for the first time), painting was probably their outstanding mutual enthusiasm. One of their conversations might have concerned the large and splendid *Shah-nameh* then being written and illustrated for the shah. Perhaps the father showed its unfinished miniatures to his son, whose Herat education would have caused him to criticize their roughness and violence. Such a discussion might explain the existence of three pages from an unfinished *Shah-nameh* identical in size with ours, one of which is the British Museum's magnificent *Sleeping Rustam.* Were these paintings put aside when Shah Isma'il canceled the commission in order to make way for a gift—the Houghton *Shah-nameh*—for his returned son? This would probably account for the corresponding page size, also for the fact that the earliest pictures for our manuscript are slightly later examples of the same style.

Whether or not these suggested circumstances for the commissioning of the Houghton manuscript are correct, we can be sure that it was begun soon after the prince's arrival in Tabriz. Such miniatures as *The feast of Sadeh* (page 93) and *Tahmuras defeats the divs* (page 97), which are still strikingly like the *Sleeping Rustam,* seem to be attempts by Sultan Muhammad himself to convert the youthful connoisseur from his classical Herat tastes to the wilder idiom of his father's court. To a degree, the artist succeeded. The Houghton *Shah-nameh* contains many similarly lively miniatures that would not be present had the young patron not been amused. But the eager youth was not to be dissuaded from the less earthy, more refined art of Herat. The very next pictures in the *Shah-nameh,* as we determine the time sequence of their painting, are those that conform to Bihzadian taste and are identical in many respects to the smaller, less elaborate pictures painted by Sultan Muhammad and his circle for the *Guy u Chawgan.* A further salute to Bihzad can be seen in *Zahhak is told his fate* (page 105), whose minuteness of scale, logical ground plan, delicately balanced palette, and naturalistic human proportions might at first baffle the attributionist. It is only when one looks closely at such characterizations as the courtiers and the gatekeeper in the right background that Sultan Muhammad's authorship becomes clear.

At the same time that Sultan Muhammad was absorbing the Herat master's idiom he was painting pictures in a fresh version of his earlier manner. A new synthesis was emerging, one suited to the Herat-educated prince who in 1524 inherited his father's brilliant atelier. Sultan Muhammad soon overcame his discomfort at having to adjust his broad and animated manner to one that may at first have seemed finicking. Now he produced pictures such as *Zahhak slays Birmayeh* (page 109), in which he painted the same blissfully silly and wisely dumb animals we met in the foreground of his *Feast of Sadeh* (page 93), but with a new fineness and concern for texture and proportion. And in this same picture his flair for trees and other vegetation, so notable in his *Sleeping Rustam,* is reasserted with gains in refinement and yet no less of poetry or vigor.

At this time, too, Sultan Muhammad must have been working on his masterpiece, *The court of Gayumars,* the painting before which his fellow artists hung their heads. Lovingly painted over a long period of time, this picture epitomizes the synthesis of Timurid and Turkman art. Its refinement of detail and psychological characterization may even surpass Bihzad's, and its dramatic impact recalls the tension we noted in the mid-fourteenth-century *Shah-nameh* page (FIGURE 4). But even if one turns this page into an art-historical romp through all sorts of motifs from the school of Tabriz—linking its lions to the Turkman album pages and its monkeys to a series in a fourteenth-century bestiary in the University Library, Istanbul—*The court of Gayumars* is not the work of a mere eclectic. Sultan Muhammad had by now absorbed the incredibly rich legacy of the royal library and workshops, and here he used it to portray all of this world and the other. The soaring rocks with their Chinese trees contain a strange and marvelous world of nature spirits. Each lapis lazuli, violet, or sulphur yellow crag harbors a secret being, or clusters of them, each merging with the next: camels, apes, lions, and people of all sorts. Sultan Muhammad seems to have set out to paint the entire world in this single miniature, and he has succeeded. If we, too, hang our heads before it, our purpose should be to look more intently at it.

During the 1520s and 30s, the period when most of the Houghton *Shah-nameh* miniatures were painted, high culture and low culture—the cerebral and the bodily or intuitive—were coming together in every area of Safavid activity. Government, poetry, religion, philosophy, and the art of these decades saw their confrontation, struggle, and eventual synthesis, with high culture in time gaining the upper hand. Changes came erratically. In politics, the low faction, represented by the Turkman soldiery, or Qizil Bash, gradually lost out after a bloody struggle. Trials and executions of religious extremists increased in number. (Anyone who now wrote as Shah Isma'il had in the early days would have been executed as a heretic.)

The arts followed a parallel course, though differences persisted between progressive artists and patrons and those who held to earlier ways. Not all patrons changed their tastes with the times, and only the more sensible, intelligent, and flexible artists could adjust to the changing cultural climate. Artists, unlike government officials or religious extremists, were relatively safe even if they could not develop with the ethos. They were not burned alive, they merely went out of fashion. Doubtless a number of painters who had worked in the visionary idiom of Shah Isma'il were forced to seek employment elsewhere, either abroad, as in India where such art was still appreciated, or in the more archaic workshops nearby, as at Shiraz.

The Houghton manuscript might be described as a battleground on which a long series of skirmishes were fought between the refined intellectuality of Bihzad's Herat and the inspired expressionism of Sultan Muhammad's Tabriz. While the trend was inevitably toward a coming together of the Timurid and Turkman elements, the artists of the manuscript did not all go into battle with the same equipment. Some bore the most newfangled weapons and used them skillfully; others were ill-equipped or just beginning to learn how to wield the new arms. Sultan Muhammad himself could enter the fray formidably: he could grasp the most up-to-date armaments, improve them, and employ them with devastating effectiveness. To a lesser degree this was also true of Mir Musavvir and Aqa Mirak, while the painters of the younger generation—Mirza Ali, Mir Sayyid Ali, and Muzaffar Ali—had been trained in the new arms from the start. Painters A through F, Sultan Muhammad's followers, were less quick to adapt. While some of them, particularly A, B, and D, progressed considerably during the years of the project, C and E, probably old dogs who could not learn new tricks, changed very little from beginning to end.

Although most of the development of early Safavid art can be traced more thoroughly in the Houghton *Shah-nameh* than in all the rest of the royal manuscripts combined, it is essential that we consider several of the others, especially because of their signatures or reliable attributions and dates. Three of these manuscripts would seem to have been made for Sam Mirza, Shah Tahmasp's brother; his name appears in one of them, and they have a stylistic kinship. One of them, a

Khamseh of Nizami in the Metropolitan Museum, was written by the Herat scribe Sultan Muhammad Nur in 1525; it now contains fifteen miniatures. Though they are unsigned, fourteen of them can be ascribed on the basis of style to the Herat painter Shaykh Zadeh or to his closely supervised followers. The other miniature, also unsigned, is undoubtedly by one of the senior painters of the Houghton manuscript, Mir Musavvir.

Another of these manuscripts, divided into two volumes, is Mir Ali-Shir Nava'i's *Anthology,* copied by Ali Hijrani at Herat in 1526/27. It is in the Bibliothèque Nationale. Of its six miniatures, five are either by Shaykh Zadeh himself or else his close followers. The sixth, a humorous hunting scene, can be ascribed stylistically to Sultan Muhammad assisted by the Houghton manuscript's Painter A.

The third manuscript of this group is a *Divan* of Hafiz in the Fogg Art Museum. Originally it contained five miniatures; one of these is now lost. The *Divan* bears neither a date nor the name of the place where it was written nor the scribe's name, but Sam Mirza's name is inscribed over a doorway in one of the manuscript's two miniatures signed by Sultan Muhammad (FIGURE 12). Another of the paintings, *A prince and a princess in a garden,* can be attributed to Sultan Muhammad. Still another, *Episode in a mosque,* is signed by Shaykh Zadeh and can be considered his masterpiece. Unlike the work of his master, Bihzad, Shaykh Zadeh's painting reveals little feeling for humanity, in which respect his character is also the opposite of Sultan Muhammad's. His vision, that of a Pascal as compared to a Montaigne, is concerned with abstract patterns and laws. Unable, it would seem, to associate himself with his players, he cannot make us feel their moods, and so we tour the surface of his paintings, enjoying their dazzling intricacies. Granted, his every line is correct, his every twist of arabesque superb.

Although all three of these manuscripts were probably copied at Herat, where Sam Mirza was governor from 1522 until 29, the miniatures were probably not all painted there. Shaykh Zadeh may well have remained in Herat, but it is unlikely that Mir Musavvir and Sultan Muhammad were there during the period in question. Probably their pictures were commissioned by the absent patron to be painted in the royal studio in Tabriz, or else they were sent as presents to his brother by Shah Tahmasp.

The earliest of the manuscripts stylistically, the 1525 *Khamseh,* is dominated by Shaykh Zadeh's interpretation of Bihzad's mode. His miniatures, with their stiff, formal characterizations, extreme two-dimensional quality, and hard-edged line, acknowledge no debt to the idiom of Tabriz. Mir Musavvir's contribution, presum-

FIGURE 12 *The celebration of Id,* by Sultan Muhammad, about 1527. Signed by the artist in cartouche on throne. From a *Divan* of Hafiz.

Fogg Art Museum, Harvard University

ably sent from Tabriz, strikes so lively a note in such company that it has sometimes been ascribed to Sultan Muhammad himself. Since Mir Musavvir is the only major Safavid artist whose miniatures reveal virtually no stylistic variation over the years of the Houghton manuscript, his picture in the *Khamseh* does not help us in dating those he painted for the *Shah-nameh*. However, his dated miniature in the *Shah-nameh* (page 169)—the only dated picture in the book—was painted fairly soon after his *Khamseh* miniature.

Shaykh Zadeh's miniatures in the *Anthology* are more open in design and considerably more inventive than his work for the *Khamseh* a year or so earlier. He now avoids the symmetrical frontality of architecture that makes his series of pavilions in the *Khamseh* rather monotonous. Furthermore, he has made a greater effort to bring his characterizations to life. He uses the same formulas as before for profiles, gestures, and other details, but he has attempted to portray human interaction, albeit with no great success. Quite probably he is here showing the influence of the new synthesis of the modes of Bihzad and Sultan Muhammad, which resulted in one of the most humanistic moments in Iranian art.

The date of the *Anthology*, 1526/27, is useful in relation to the Houghton manuscript because many of Painter A's Houghton miniatures, in most of which he was assisted by or inspired by Sultan Muhammad, are closely related to his hunting scene in the Paris manuscript. His *Rustam cleaves a witch* (page 149) is probably of about the same date as his Paris miniature, which includes a comparable earthy humor as well as similarities of landscape, figural, and animal painting.

Sultan Muhammad's three miniatures of the Fogg *Divan* must also have been painted about 1526. The artist's rendering of farce in his two signed miniatures was probably encouraged by his young patron, Sam Mirza, who was one of the leading wits in the Safavid court. The *Ode on drunkenness* illustration (FIGURE 13), a cosmic revel, combines Bihzad's subtleties of execution (the inlaid door is so infinitesimally fine that one can hardly make out the design without a lens) with the zestful abandon of his *Sleeping Rustam*. As in his Houghton masterpiece, *The court of Gayumars*, Sultan Muhammad has combined his own former manner with the elements of Bihzad's style that most appealed to him. Nothing has been lost in the blend. His sense of humor, expressed in muscular buffoonery, enables him in *The celebration of Id* to regale us with the psychological intricacies of a worldly court, where only one figure in the entire crowd (a popeyed dolt on the roof, third man from the right) takes seriously the religious purpose of the feast. It seems likely that such caricatural improvisation was especially enjoyed by

FIGURE 13 *Illustration to an ode on drunkenness*, by Sultan Muhammad, about 1527. Signed by the artist over left doorway. From the *Divan* of Hafiz.

Fogg Art Museum

گرفته ساغر عشرت فرشتهٔ رحمت
ز جرعه بر رخ حور و پری گلاب زده

the artist and by Sam Mirza when the increasing formality of Shah Tahmasp's view of life probably discouraged such high jinks closer to the royal eye.

Shaykh Zadeh's *Episode in a mosque,* painted for the *Divan* about 1527, shows that he had by now changed his style somewhat to conform to the more psychologically oriented idiom admired at the Safavid court. His admirably balanced, Mondrian-like compositions, with their precise workmanship and balanced rectangles, were losing their appeal for progressive connoisseurs. We have noted his attempts to achieve the humanism of Sultan Muhammad. These were insufficient. His star was waning. The proportion of his pictures to those of others was changing. While the generously illustrated *Khamseh* of 1525 is almost entirely his work, the *Anthology* of 1526/27 contains but five of his pictures, and in the *Divan,* where he made a huge effort to please, his paintings, in a total of five, are outnumbered three to two.

By 1527 the royal Safavid school was excluding painters who could not go beyond the mode that had prevailed at the court of Shah Isma'il, and those like Shaykh Zadeh who persisted in repeating the Herat formulas of a generation before. Shaykh Zadeh's work is not found in the Houghton manuscript or in any other volume known to us that was illustrated for the Safavids later than the Fogg *Divan.* We next find him in a *Haft Manzar* of Hatifi copied by Mir Ali at Bukhara in 1538 for Sultan Abd al-Aziz, the ruler of the Uzbeks from 1530 to 40. One of his miniatures for this manuscript, which is in the Freer Gallery of Art, is inscribed: "This was painted by the most insignificant of the sultanic servants, Shaykh Zadeh." Its style harks back to the 1525 *Khamseh,* though it is still more archaic. At Bukhara Shaykh Zadeh's rather dry interpretation of the Bihzadian style was to be the mode for years to come.

The Houghton manuscript shows clearly that Shah Tahmasp had come to enjoy elements of his father's taste. If he had once admired Bihzadian art exclusively, this attitude changed soon after his return to Tabriz. Bihzad himself, due to age and failing eyesight, ceased to be a major power and did not paint for the Houghton *Shah-nameh* even though, according to Dust Muhammad, he lived on until 1535/36. A manuscript of Sharaf al-Din's *Zafar-nameh,* copied by the royal scribe Sultan Muhammad Nur in 1528, appears to be one of the old master's later projects. Although it has not been possible for me to examine this manuscript's twenty-four miniatures (the manuscript is in the library of the Gulistan Palace, Teheran), those that may be seen in reproductions do not seem to be by any of the artists who worked on the Houghton manuscript. Several of these miniatures contain elements of design ascribable to Bihzad, and the compositions suggest that he planned them. If so, he had been considerably demoted, for historical manuscripts such as this *Zafar-nameh* were seldom commissioned from the best available talent.

Shah Tahmasp's youthful sense of humor survived military invasions from east and west as well as such episodes as his being ignored or deserted by his so-called followers, and the occasion when, at the age of thirteen, he was compelled to execute an enemy with a bow and arrow. The survival is demonstrated by one of the most human and appealing documents of his reign (FIGURE 14), a candid glimpse of the royal household staff, signed by the shah himself and inscribed by him to his favorite (and only uterine) brother, Bahram Mirza. The miniature occupies a position of honor—the opening page, folio 1 verso—of the album

FIGURE 14
The royal household staff, by Shah Tahmasp, second quarter 16th century. Signed by the artist at top, beneath inscription.

Topkapu Seray Museum Library H. 2154

assembled by Dust Muhammad (page 16). The names of the staff are inscribed at the top of the painting and include such affectionate appellations as Karpuz ("Melon") Sultan for the jolly fellow in the lower row with the appropriately shaped belly. A drawing by the shah of this same retainer, apparently a comical royal butler, is on the next page of the same album, signed with the same formula ("The Refuge of the World") we find in the shah's copy of Arifi's *Guy u Chawgan.* Both the painting and drawing can be assigned to the late 1520s or early 30s, and while there is evidently no work in the Houghton manuscript by this royal hand, many of its miniatures evoke the same spirit. The shah who could caricature Karpuz Sultan would also enjoy Mir Musavvir's gentler representations of obesity—for example, the courtier at the far right, shown in profile the better to reveal his roundness, in *Zal receives Mihrab's homage at Kabul* (page 129). One wonders whether this may not even be our friend Karpuz Sultan.

Only a lively, fun-loving young patron could have appreciated the full range of the Houghton *Shah-nameh.* Its changing moods, from visionary seriousness to slapstick comedy, its ascents to such pinnacles of quality as *The court of Gayumars,* its descents to pages that seem—by comparison—mere daubs, and its stylistic variety make it a record of the growth of Shah Tahmasp's personality. The book's two hundred and fifty-eight miniatures do not form a consistently structured ensemble; rather, they can be seen as a sporadically conceived personal chronicle, into which are locked almost as many intimate anecdotes as there are verses of the epic. If only Shah Tahmasp could come alive to recount them for us!

The political upheavals of the 1520s and 30s, when the shah was frequently on the move, must have contributed to the irregular growth of the *Shah-nameh.* Some of the artists probably accompanied their patron on his journeys. Others either remained in Tabriz or went to their villages on holiday or to escape a threatened Ottoman invasion. A group of Painter C's miniatures apparently met with accident while being brought in a small pile for inspection: all were folded, causing creases in the same unsightly pattern, before they finally reached the binder.

Sultan Muhammad and Mir Musavvir must already have been master artists at the time of Shah Isma'il's accession. Painters of the next generation worked as apprentices to these older men who had formed the new synthesis. By the early 1530s a new cadre had reached the fledgling stage. Although still very young men, they were able to accept important commissions for major manuscripts. Sultan Muhammad's son, Mirza Ali, may well have painted his first large "solo" pictures for the Houghton volume. The first of these in order of appearance, though probably not the earliest in date, is *Firdowsi's parable of the ship of Shi'ism.* This can be identified as Mirza Ali's work on the basis of its affinities to his reliably attributed paintings in the British Museum's fragmentary *Khamseh* of 1539–43. Boldly composed and brilliantly colored, *The ship of Shi'ism* brings to mind Shaykh Zadeh's version of the Bihzadian mode rather than the mode of Bihzad himself, but perhaps the second-generation Safavid masters found the style of the second-generation Bihzadian easier to grasp. *The ship of Shi'ism* is so markedly akin to miniatures by Shaykh Zadeh, whose formulas for water, ships, fish, and birds it repeats, one wonders if some personal relationship did not exist between these artists. Did Shaykh Zadeh come to Tabriz and instruct Mirza Ali? May the younger man have gone to Herat for part of his apprenticeship? On the other hand, it is conceivable that Mirza Ali's borrowings can be explained by his close study of paintings brought to Tabriz. He need never have met the painter himself.

Nushirvan receives an embassy from the king of Hind (page 180), one of Mirza Ali's most ambitious paintings in the *Shah-nameh,* combines ingredients from most of the sources we have considered, in which respect it typifies work by a young, easily influenced painter of the second generation. While the figures are beginning to take on traits that appear in Mirza Ali's more mature miniatures, they still owe much to Shaykh Zadeh, particularly in their jutting jaws, sadly drooping eyes, and oddly flattened profiles. The plane tree bears a debt to Shaykh Zadeh, too, in its sharply outlined, flat pattern, but it owes still more to Sultan Muhammad and to his sources—to the breezy vegetation of paintings in Turkman Tabriz, to the style of the *Khavaran-nameh* of 1477 and the Herat *Jamal u Jalal* of 1502/03. If Mirza Ali's courtiers, musicians, and attendants reveal Bihzad's restrained psychological concerns, they also tell of Sultan Muhammad's bolder and more humorous eye for mankind. His influence, too, accounts for the turbulent rhythm of the composition, which bursts across the page, and for the lively dragon and phoenix design we find on a curtain.

To learn as much as we can about the latest and most progressive miniatures in the Houghton *Shah-nameh* we must turn to the British Museum's *Khamseh* of 1539–43. This book, surely the one referred to by Dust Muhammad in the Bahram Mirza album along with the Houghton manuscript, was copied by the famed scribe Shah Mahmud Nishapuri, who may also have penned the *Shah-nameh.* Shah Tahmasp's name appears in the introduction to the *Khamseh* and on a palace wall in one of its miniatures. In its present state the volume contains fourteen contemporary miniatures and three added in the late seventeenth century by the artist Muhammad Zaman. On the whole, the condition of the paintings is less good than in the Houghton volume. While they have suffered less from pigment oxidation (generally a curable disorder), a number of them have been retouched. Unable to restrain his brush, Muhammad Zaman transformed sixteenth-century beauties, both courtly and angelic, into up-to-date ones, giving some of them Europeanized faces. Probably because of excessive handling, the *Khamseh* must have been in somewhat sorry repair when it was reworked. Whatever the reason, most of the miniatures were given new figural borders in late seventeenth-century style, far less fine than the original borders. Several of these replacements are all too apparent, especially around the miniatures of irregular outline. The overzealous conservators were probably also responsible for the removal of several of the book's miniatures. One of these, *Khosrow Parviz battling Bahram Chubineh,* attributable to Mir Sayyid Ali, is now in the Royal Scottish Museum, Edinburgh. Two more, mutilated by being cut in half, are in the Fogg Art Museum: *Alexander gives an entertainment* and *A conference between the tribes of Nawfal and Layla.* These also are by Mir Sayyid Ali.

One painting in the *Khamseh,* folio 15 verso, contains a wall inscribed with the date 1538 and a partly obliterated signature. Many of the others, including one of the Fogg paintings, are inscribed with the names Sultan Muhammad, Aqa Mirak, Mirza Ali, Mir Sayyid Ali, and Muzaffar Ali. With one exception (the name Mirza Ali in the replaced border of folio 48 verso), the names seem to have been written by the same later hand. As we have seen, original signatures are rare in Safavid painting; and the patron, not to mention the artists, would hardly have allowed even the most admired of librarians to sully his miniatures with script. While we may object to the anonymous connoisseur's impudence and his not very elegant calligraphy, his attributions in the *Khamseh* have proven wholly reliable, both for internal consistency and against other signed work.

Unlike the Houghton *Shah-nameh,* the *Khamseh* is unified and harmonious. It never contained the plenitude of illustrations that are both the strength and weakness of the *Shah-nameh.* Furthermore, its known paintings are all by major masters. If our painters A through F painted for it, they did so as anonymous assistants to the more progressive and admired men. This indicates that by 1539 insistence upon technical refinement and courtly "good taste" had put a limit to the number of illustrations for even the most royal of manuscripts. High painting had driven out low.

The ethos was moving yet higher, in politics as in art. Orthodoxy was the order of the day. In 1537 the shah and his grand vizier, Qadi-yi Jahan (his former lala, fellow paintings enthusiast, and the recipient of the 1523/24 *Guy u Chawgan*), stopped in Teheran to try and sentence extremist Sufis. Like the wilder, humbler artists, these Sufis would have been admired previously. In 1541 a campaign was conducted in Khuzistan to combat similarly extreme political and religious elements. In poetry, too, the ecstatic and visionary were ceasing to be in vogue. But should one expect Shah Tahmasp the patron to hold different views from Shah Tahmasp the ruler?

The spirit of the *Khamseh* is to some extent exemplified by the sophistication of its painted characters, who can be taken as the beaus ideal of their period. We are seeing a second- or even a third-generation court. The first had won the battles and seized the power. Now that the power has been defended and secured, the time had come to enjoy it. Most of the people we meet in the *Khamseh* are exquisites. Princesses and princes, pages and grooms—all appear to have been sewn into their sumptuous garments by an army of tailors. Rich stuffs are all about. Gold thrones, delicately worked bow cases (even the weapons are now precious works of art), and beautiful salvers spread with delicacies set the mood. To stir the hearts of the sons of brave warriors, princesses sound their harps in the hunting field. Dragons and phoenixes, which once had boldly loped and soared, now sinuously adorn.

But the earlier generation lived on, doubtless lamenting "the good old days," and it was not exclusively represented by the gruff old soldiers gently ridiculed in the *Khamseh.* Senior artists such as Sultan Muhammad were still important painters. The new synthesis found in the *Khamseh* retains undercurrents of the ecstatic. For instance, Sultan Muhammad's great *Ascent of the Prophet* is as true a descendant of the Turkman idiom, of the *Jamal u Jalal* style, and of the *Sleeping Rustam* as it is of Bihzad. The artist had become an "underground" Sufi, a suavely disguised wildman-saint. As the Prophet soars into the heavens on his human-headed mount, Buraq (FIGURE 15), we see in the distance, nearer than the infinite starry sky, a radiant golden moon surrounded by a light blue aura. Muhammad rises above wispy clouds filled with dragons and grotesques, perhaps intended as the last fringes of earthliness, through which worshipful angels fly, bearing a lamp, an offering of heavenly fire, and an incense burner. Other angels bearing other gifts compose a flickering oval around the Prophet, while the chief angel, perhaps Gabriel, beckons. Golden illumination, as energetic as electric sparks and hot as fire, emanates from the Prophet. Yet for all its mystical potential, the ascent is put before us in plausibly concrete terms. To the Safavid observer it must have linked his world to the one depicted: the Prophet wears the Safavid headgear (now slightly defaced), and Buraq's blanket and the angels' trappings are represented as the best that the royal Safavid workshops could produce. Moreover, the fabulous Buraq is thoroughly believable, space is convincingly defined, and all proportions are credibly natural. Only the spirit of the picture is otherworldly as it carries the beholder closer to heaven.

Sultan Muhammad's latest picture for the *Shah-nameh, The execution of Zahhak* (page 117), is so similar in style to his miniatures for the *Khamseh* that it cannot have been painted more than a few years earlier. While still containing traces of Turkman inspiration, the dragonlike clouds, the inhabited mountain, the sinister executioner, and the elegantly accoutered horses belong more to the world of the *Khamseh* than to the strata of his earliest paintings for the *Shah-nameh.*

Another painter who worked on both the Houghton manuscript and the *Khamseh,* Aqa Mirak, seems to have been considerably younger than Sultan Muhammad, though not of the second generation. The earliest work ascribable to him is

FIGURE 15 *The ascent of the Prophet,* by Sultan Muhammad, from a *Khamseh* of Nizami dated 1539–43.

in the 1523/24 *Guy u Chawgan;* his latest pictures are in a manuscript of Jami's *Haft Awrang,* dated between 1556 and 65, in the Freer Gallery of Art. Aqa Mirak was an admired portraitist as well as a boon companion of the shah, whom he may have depicted in his *Firdowsi encounters the court poets of Ghazna* (page 80), the first picture in our manuscript. Such opening miniatures traditionally included portraits of their patrons, and the figure here, standing somewhat removed from the others, is clothed with particular splendor. Aqa Mirak's miniatures for the *Khamseh* include two more representations of the same striking individual, whose long, slightly drooping nose and less than strong chin are consistent with our appraisal of Shah Tahmasp's personality. In both the *Khamseh* paintings the individual is fittingly portrayed as Khosrow, a revered legendary figure whose name is synonymous with royalty.

Whether or not Aqa Mirak's gathering of poets includes a royal portrait, the picture is one of the latest he painted for the *Shah-nameh.* On the basis of style it can be assigned to the years just prior to the *Khamseh,* which may account for the slightly softer, more youthful countenance of the beardless young shah as compared to the two Khosrows. This again demonstrates how long a time it took to complete the Houghton volume. If the shah and Sultan Muhammad had at first supposed that the book would progress from beginning to end in a smooth succession of stylistically similar miniatures, they soon must have discovered otherwise. However quickly the artists worked, they could keep up neither with the demands of the project in terms of quantity nor with the rapid changes of style taking place in the patron's picture-conscious court. Although we surmise that the book was begun soon after the future shah's return to Tabriz in 1522, its terminal date is harder to estimate. The work would seem to have continued during most, if not all, of the years of the shah's serious devotion to painting. He was wont to add to it whenever the spirit moved him. One envisions him turning its pages in the royal library and suddenly deciding that Mirza Ali or Aqa Mirak should paint another miniature for it, perhaps to replace one that had begun to cloy or bore. Thus, as we have noted, the first few paintings in the book are among the latest chronologically, while the last picture in the book, a battle scene by Dust Muhammad (folio 745 verso), can be dated on the grounds of style to not later than the early 1530s.

The resultant chaos of styles, each a stage in the royal aesthetic and spiritual progress, symbolizes the shah's groping search for a mode of expression in keeping with his changing philosophy. What at first glance might seem to exemplify unevenness, confusion, and poor planning is in fact a monument built by the most gifted Safavid artists to record their energetic, deeply concerned patron's growing tastes. If the British Museum's *Khamseh* reveals the mature height attained by the shah in partnership with his painters, the *Shah-nameh* shows us all the steps, including a few pitfalls, on the way to the summit. At times, the by-products of a struggle surpass the goal in interest.

Shah Tahmasp's attitude toward painting began with an immature boy's admiration for the mode of Bihzad, to which he was exposed at Herat. Upon returning to Tabriz, the still very impressionable prince was made aware of the quite different school patronized by his father. The two strands met, merged, and rose to the synthesized style that culminated in the later masterpieces for the *Shah-nameh* and the *Khamseh.* Shah Tahmasp came to admire art that was technically fully accomplished, intellectual, subtle, and increasingly resistant to new ideas—an art that tended, in short, toward the academic. Painting, to which the boy and youth had been so devoted, once represented his personal search for fulfillment. While young, he had had a compulsive need for painting; as a man he was under no further obligation to be its loving patron. His emotions required other outlets. Whereas Sultan Muhammad achieved true satisfaction through his creativity in painting, the shah did not. In immaturity he had been able to pour his feelings into the molding of a school of art, but his painful, thwarted struggle for maturity failed to bring complete happiness. Instead of leading to a livelier palace of joyful gardens, where fear could be transmuted into love, the way ended in sand and ashes. Shah Tahmasp could love neither man nor art, neither the living nor the dead. The years of his life that should have been the most happy, responsible, and creative were, instead, bitter. He sought refuge in orthodoxy. The natural love that is allotted to every person had dried up in him. Only hate and lust remained, and these could be controlled only by rigid self-discipline and deadly and deadening self-incarceration. After 1556 Shah Tahmasp only once left the area of the royal palace at Qazvin. Although he had been prone to guilts during most of his life, his renunciations of wine and other pleasures increased during the middle years. Frequently, his puritanical moods followed nightmares. In all likelihood, these miseries stemmed from psychological wounds sustained years before. His life was the tragedy of a man who was given more than his share of worldly power but had, in infancy, been denied love.

As compensation, he turned to art. The most convincing proofs for this channeling of devotion are the paintings themselves. Beyond these, there are the literary references. These must be evaluated properly, of course. For some of the writers, particularly those in the employ of the Safavid house, the motives may have been flattery. For others, as with the comments of Sam Mirza, his sometimes jealous and ever rival brother, a word of mere recognition of talent or interest can be considered understatement.

Qadi Ahmad, probably a truthful reporter, tells us that "this exalted Majesty was greatly inclined toward this wonder-working art, in which he was master. . . . At first Shah Tahmasp was greatly drawn to learning the nasta'liq script and painting, and spent his time on these. He became an incomparable master rising above all the artists in drawing and painting . . . [and] deserved a hundred thousand praises and approvals." Sadiqi Beg, a major artist and writer on the arts of the late sixteenth century, also a contentious and rather mutinous spirit not likely to stretch the truth in the direction of flattery, had this to say: "Such was his competence in the field of painting that the leading masters in the library could never put the final touches to their work before submitting it for his majesty's correction and approval."

Ali, the Ottoman man of letters, wrote as an honestly impressed court member of a competing power. While some of his remarks were intended less to inform than to praise his own patron at the expense of the Safavid ruler, he was surely not dissimulating when he wrote that Shah Tahmasp was a "master painter (*naqqash-i-ustad*), his artistry was Bihzad-like in its creativity. This stems as much from his apprenticeship with 'Abd al-Aziz as from a natural delight he derived from his fine connoisseurship of drawing and painting." Further on, in describing another patron, the shah's nephew, Sultan Ibrahim Mirza, for whom the *Haft Awrang* of 1556–65 was made, Ali refers to both him and Shah Tahmasp as having "the rare recognition previously reserved for such princely precursors in the arts as Sultan Uvays Bahadur, epigon of the glorious Jalayirid dynasty, and Mirza Baysunghur, worthy scion of the line of Timur. The refinement of technique and the peerless accomplishment displayed by these Safavid princes in the realm of art have become universally recognized as truly unique."

Elsewhere the same Ottoman writer, who sincerely admired the shah's artistry, could not resist gossiping. He recounted an anecdote concerning one of the shah's favorite page boys, who was carried off by the shah's own master in painting, Abd al-Aziz, and his pupil Ali-Ashgar. This sordid episode involved the theft of the royal seal, its use on forged documents, an escape and a chase, the capture and imprisonment of the criminals, and their eventual de-nosing and de-earing by the infuriated shah's own hand. The boy was forgiven—and Abd al-Aziz's artistry was demonstrated when he carved himself a new nose in wood that was said to be an improvement over the one he had lost to the royal knife.

This incident took place prior to 1550, when Sam Mirza also mentioned it. By now this brother's comments on Shah Tahmasp's connoisseurship in art were delivered in the past tense. Other writers speak of his gradual loss of interest and even rejection of art. Qadi Ahmad, for instance, alludes to his change of mind in relation to the scribe Shah Mahmud Zarin-qalam: "For some time he resided in the capital, Tabriz. . . . In the end, when [Shah Tahmasp], having wearied of the field of calligraphy and painting, occupied himself with important affairs of state, with the well-being of the country and the tranquility of his subjects, the maulana [master], having obtained leave, came to Holy Masshad . . . [where] he lived for

FIGURE 16 *Majnun visiting Layla,* by Shaykh Muhammad, from a *Haft Awrang* of Jami dated between 1556 and 65.

Freer Gallery of Art, Washington

some 20 years." As Qadi Ahmad also tells us that the calligrapher died in Mashhad in 1564/65, the time of the shah's disaffection must have been about 1544/45.

The last great surviving manuscript of Shah Tahmasp's reign, the Freer Gallery of Art's *Haft Awrang,* while not made for him, in many respects reflects his spirit between 1556 and 65, when it was created. A miniature from this manuscript by Shaykh Muhammad illustrates this phase (FIGURE 16). We approach it cautiously, as a scientist might peer through a microscope at his perfect specimen of malignant tissue—for of its sort this picture is superb. The plot is confusing and apparently lost amidst proliferating smutty episodes. Jaded crones, evil servants and duennas, depraved girls and boys make up the cast. The camels have the look of painted-up bawds, and the horses are fit mounts only for the demon lover. This brilliant work of a great, if tormented, artist evokes something like the ambiance of Proust. There is wit here, and it is totally in keeping with the players—the wit of a keenly observant courtier, part moralist, part participant in the revels. He noted that the wine was vinegar, but he drank it.

Not surprisingly, the picture ultimately moves us much as does Sultan Muhammad's *Gabriel announcing the apotheosis of Ali* (FIGURE 8), and this by almost the same means. Space in the earlier picture (note the relationship of the canal to the trees) was no more logical than here, where horses and camels pop up from nowhere. People in both paintings stand in impossible relationships to one another, and proportions are weirdly inconsistent. In both, intellectuality and serenity are to the same extent lacking, or present. But while the earlier picture is simple, innocent, and eager, rising toward the summit, the later one is complex guilt-ridden, and willfully heading for oblivion. The sense of body, which lends empathy, has been regained, but it now brings pain rather than wholesomeness. In both paintings, too, the color is strong—in the *Gabriel* bright and fresh, with unripe rawness, in the *Majnun* admixed with black, which lends a cloying, overripe bittersweetness.

A formal comparison of the two is also revealing. The first is sturdy in composition, well knit, muscular, and in effect youthful; the second is sprawling, flaccidly old. Despite the arresting, violent lozenges, diagonals, and stripes in the tent patterns, the total effect is one of outward spinning motion. Elements of design are not pulling together as in the *Gabriel;* they are being dispersed. Art is going to seed, and the centrifugal power before us is the graphic symbolization of the wind that scatters. With luck, a few seeds will land on fertile soil and be nurtured. This is one of art's natural ways of reproducing itself. From miniatures such as this a new cycle may commence.

During the years following his great period of patronage Shah Tahmasp rose to extraordinary heights of political activity, especially in the early 1550s, after which his mood seems to have soured. He was like a once sparkling fountain that had spouted good wine and now trickled clouded water. The generous, fun-loving, amiable shah froze. Within his mind there still existed the laughing, occasionally ecstatic youth of the past, now struck deaf, dumb, and blind—a youth self-imprisoned by a somber internal squad of cranky but efficient hollow men: an officious general who could erect fresh towers of skulls; a guilt-ravaged puritan in terror of contamination by worldly filth or religious heresy; a jealous unloved lover; and an unyielding miser eager to tax, whose apparent generosity concealed avarice.

Occasionally the inner boy awoke. Flickers of life broke through, even in the clinically immaculate palace of the shah's self-incarceration. This once exuberant, now middle-aged, king was a lonely, still immature boy, playing fearfully at being a great shah. Unable to accept himself as a man, he could not grow up and be accepted by others. A terrible internal struggle resulted, a tug of war between the barely living boy and the squad of automatons he had created as a simulacrum. When the boy won, a celebration took place, as when his favorite nephew, Sultan Ibrahim Mirza, the patron of the *Haft Awrang,* married his eldest daughter. But the poor fellow was doomed to be overpowered by the dour "men" inside, who stirred up envy and hate. If in a moment of warm generosity the shah appointed Ibrahim, his inner boy's comrade, governor of Mashhad, the move was eventually countered by jealousy. Or, when Sultan Ibrahim was allowed to employ the remaining royal painters for his great manuscript, a coldly automatic envy wanted the artists back, even though they could not be given regular work in the palace, where joy of all sorts had been banished in the name of orthodoxy.

Although there was intense friendship between uncle and nephew, the relationship was hard. Shah Tahmasp gave, Ibrahim accepted. Then the shah, torn between love and hate, would demand his gift returned. The nephew was baffled and angered. He wrote verses ridiculing his eccentric uncle. Once, when the shah had fired all his court musicians and ordered one of them in particular to be slain, Ibrahim prepared a subterranean chamber to protect him. There was guilt always. The shah's tormented subconscious, never at peace with the rest of his mind, if silenced by day, could harangue at night. In a dream, his conscience proclaimed that he should revoke all taxes not justified by religious law. Sales taxes and tolls were remitted on the following day.

These were gloomy years. In a society where one man rules, that man's moods prevail within the range of his influence. While the very energetic shah of earlier years had truly dominated Iran, the ingrown, self-imprisoned, self-weakened shah let the system muddle on. Perhaps he withdrew intuitively, to hurt less. Within the circle of the court his struggle against fear cast deep shadows. When strange green lights were seen in the northern sky in 1572, only a pessimistic interpretation was possible. Poets who had once proclaimed victories or lauded love now sang dirges, by royal command, about the gory agonies of Shi'ah martyrs. Love had to go underground, like the hidden singer escaped from the shah's wrath.

Old age often brings consolation to the troubled. Shah Tahmasp was one of those. All his life he had been prone to illnesses at times of crisis. His period of greatest activity was preceded by physical disorder. Now, in 1574, he was again struck down. This time he appears to have gained richly from the sickness that sapped him of strength but simultaneously gave him peace. The insecure inner boy was magically transmuted into a contented old man. The shah, who had never before been able to give with true generosity, could now at least receive in good spirit. He had entered the time of forgetfulness that lessened the sting of previous miseries. Now he could forgive and enjoy the innocent, loving delights reserved for the very young and the very old. Like a child, he no longer needed to depend upon canny logic or even coherent thought. He could be guided by intuition, which told him to accept, to love, and to enjoy. Illness and time had forced him into selflessness.

These last years must have been inactive but happy, probably the happiest since early childhood. There was no compulsion for him to do anything. He simply stayed in the palace or puttered in the garden, always a haven for contentment, perhaps accompanied by his many grandchildren. While this period was not creative in a tangible sense, the prematurely old man must have regained his sensitivity to people and to things that had been lost during his years of self-denial.

With the shah's old age, prospective heirs to the throne and their supporters gathered in Qazvin. One of them was Sultan Ibrahim Mirza, who at last became a fully trusted administrator in the innermost circle of the court. Now an active and ambitious man of thirty-four, this son of the shah's only revered brother must have spent many happy hours with his uncle. A poet, musician, inventor, and—as we have seen—notable enthusiast of painting, Ibrahim Mirza was good company.

We can only speculate about Shah Tahmasp's last two years, during which so little apparently occurred. In all probability this was again a creative time for painting, but we have no complete major manuscript to demonstrate this. Sultan Ibrahim was in the position once again to employ the leading artists, and it can be assumed that the old shah regained his enthusiasm for art, sparked by his nephew's interest. A double-page landscape by Mirza Ali, who was still one of the major artists, must have been painted at this time (FIGURE 17). In it we find the artist's usual concern for courtly personalities, depicted with gentle toleration of their

FIGURE 17
Hunting scenes, double-page miniature by Mirza Ali, about 1570.

Metropolitan Museum of Art (left-hand page), Rogers Fund, 1912. Museum of Fine Arts, Boston (right-hand page), Francis Bartlett Donation & Special Picture Fund, 1914

foibles. Comparing these scenes to the one in the *Haft Awrang,* we are struck by the absence of pain and bitterness. Now that the shah's personality had mellowed, Shaykh Muhammad's acid characterizations were passé. In their place we find sympathy and understanding. The sinuous line, sinister-seeming in the Freer miniature, has here taken on the gentle curvilinear motion of growth.

The shah died on May 4, 1576, aged sixty-two. The power factions that had lain waiting in the court fought openly in the palace compound. It was claimed that Sultan Ibrahim had attempted to force the shah to designate him his heir. For this he was imprisoned and executed by Shah Isma'il II. Before he died he wrote an accusing letter that in itself would have guaranteed the impossibility of pardon. After he was killed at the age of thirty-seven, his wife, Princess Gawhar-Sultan Khanum, ordered brought to her a great album he had assembled. According to Qadi Ahmad, who must have known it, the album contained "writings of masters and paintings of Maulana Bihzad and others." The chronicler praised it in verse:

> From the point of view of cleanness and distinction
> Nothing but the soul would find a place in it.
> Because of the images of flowers and shapes of birds
> It was a Paradise unspoiled by the autumn wind.
> Thousands of its roses and tulips, stems and petals,
> Were immune from the harm of storms and hail.
> Youths represented with sunlike faces, in shame,
> Had closed their lips in their conversation.
> All of them united in war and peace,
> Not like the dwellers of the world full of hypocrisy and dishonor!
> Day and night companions of the same quarters,
> Men devoid of discord in their communion!

When it was brought to her, the princess "washed out the album with water, that is should not fall under the eyes of Shah Isma'il."

Thus passed two creative patrons, one young, one old, whose lives were bound together.

PAGES FROM
THE HOUGHTON
SHAH-NAMEH

برسم
کتابخانه السلطان الاعظم
والخاقان الاعدل الاکرم
السلطان بن السلطان بن السلطان ابو
المظفر السلطان شاه طهماسب الحسینی
الصفوی بهادر خان خلد
الله تعالی ملکه وسلطانه
علی العالمین عدله

Dedicatory page

16

RECTO This richly ornamented rosette, like a sunburst in the manuscript, is inscribed. In the upper cartouche one reads:

In His Name, the Most Praised and Most Exalted!

IN THE ROSETTE:

Commissioned for the Library of the most mighty Sultan, and the most just and beneficent Khaqan [Grand Khan], sultan, son and grandson of sultans, Abu'l-Muzaffar [The Victorious], Sultan Shah Tahmasp, of Huseyni and Safavid descent, Bahadur [The Valiant] Khan. May God, the Most Exalted, perpetuate his realm and his rule, and diffuse ...

IN THE LOWER CARTOUCHE:

... his justice and his benevolence throughout the world!

درجواب کفت اکر توانم بکویم و الا زحمت ببرم

چون عارض تو ماه نباشد روشن | مانند رخت کل نبود در کلشن
مژکانت همی کذر کند از جوشن | مانند سنان کیو در جنک پشن

ایشان کیفیت جنک کیو و پشن پرسیدند تقریری خوش کرد چنانچه مجموع فضل او را مسلم داشتند بمصاحبت و مباحثت با این طایفه مستأنس شد و شعرا او را امتحانات میکردند و هر لحظه بدیهه و لطیفهٔ دیکر در میان می آوردند و فردوسی در میدان بدیهه بغایت چابک سوار بود

چو کشتی باسب بدیهه سوار | برآوردی از خیل فکرت دمار
برمح سخن در صف ارتجال | شکستی بیک حمله قلب رجال

وچون شعرای غزنین ارتقای ابوالقاسم بر مدارج فنون هنر معلوم کردند راه مداخلت مجلس سلطان و طرق معرفت او با حجاب آستان مسدود میداشتند تا او را با ماهک که از ندمای مجلس سلطان بود ملاقات افتاد و حبل الفت و رشتهٔ مودت مبرم و محکم کردانید

Firdowsi encounters the court poets of Ghazna

The author of the *Shah-nameh* (standing at the lower left), recently arrived in Ghazna from his native city of Tus, has come upon three famous poets (the seated bearded trio). Disturbed by the stranger's intrusion and fearful that he may be a boorish puritan (for he has just been seen publicly performing his prayers), the poets try to avoid Firdowsi's company by explaining that they are the poets of the sultan, Mahmud, and that only poets are welcome here. They put Firdowsi to a test, demanding that he supply the fourth line of a quatrain, which they artfully devise with a difficult rhyme. Firdowsi delivers so brilliantly that the poets are compelled to accept him.

The circumstances surrounding this meeting are ironical. Sultan Mahmud had been collecting the ancient records and oral traditions surviving from pre-Islamic Iran, and had made known his desire to have the best talent of the age turn this raw material into a unified poetical work. The three poets were among the leading contenders for the commission. What no one in Ghazna yet knew was that Firdowsi, in provincial Tus, had already become occupied with this very task. Indeed, his main purpose in coming to the capital was to obtain the patronage of the sultan for his *Shah-nameh*. The episode depicted here led to an introduction to the sultan, who perceived Firdowsi's talent and commissioned him to write the book. Unfortunately, the patron did not appreciate what was done for him until too late. According to tradition, he eventually sent a generous gift to the poet, but the caravan bearing it arrived just as Firdowsi's body was being taken to the graveyard.

7

RECTO

This sumptuously colored miniature, the first in the manuscript, can be attributed to Aqa Mirak, a close companion of Shah Tahmasp and an artist noted for his portraits. Stylistically, it would seem to be one of the latest pictures made for the book.

The splendid figure looking in on the tenth-century poets' picnic may well be Shah Tahmasp, the patron of this copy of the *Shah-nameh.*

Firdowsi quietly awaits the welcome of his fellow poets.

Firdowsi's parable of the ship of Shi'ism

At the outset of the *Shah-nameh* the poet explains his philosophy and religious beliefs. Here he envisions a parable of doomed passengers aboard seventy ships bearing the seventy religions of mankind (Negroes, Chinese, and Europeans can be seen among the passengers and crews). The largest and fairest of the ships bears the holy family of the Shi'ah sect, and on this one Firdowsi (in this copy of the poem prepared for a Shi'ite patron) has booked passage. Aware that all the ships must founder in the stormy sea of eternity, the poet reflects that even so he can clutch the helping hands of his ever-present saviors: the Prophet, his son-in-law and successor, Ali (both seated beneath the canopy), and Ali's sons Hasan and Huseyn (the figures nearest them). The holy ones are haloed by their auras of sanctity and veiled—either to confine their blinding effulgence or to compromise with orthodox iconoclasm. Further, they are wearing the Safavid headdress: turban wound around a baton.

18

VERSO This painting is an early work by Mirza Ali, the son of Sultan Muhammad and a contemporary of Shah Tahmasp. It must have been added to the book in the mid-1530s. One can find in the ships, water, and fish the influence of Shaykh Zadeh, a painter who himself did no work for the *Shah-nameh* and was out of favor after about 1527.

منم بندهٔ اهل بیت نبی
چو هفتاد کشتی برو ساخته
محمد درو اندرون با علی
ستایندهٔ خاک پای وصی
همه بادبانها برافراخته
همان اهل بیت نبی و ولی
حکیم این جهان را چو دریا نهاد
یکی پهن کشتی بسان عروس
برانگیخته موج ازو تند باد
بیاراسته همچو چشم خروس
بدانست کو موج خواهد زدن
همانا که باشد مرا دستگیر
اگر چشم داری بدیگر سرای
کس از غرقه بیرون نخواهد شدن
خداوند تاج و لوا و سریر
بنزد نبی و وصی گیر جای
خردمند کز دور دریا بدید
بدل گفت اگر با نبی و وصی
خداوند جوی می و انگبین
گرت زین بد آید گناه منست
کرانه نه پیدا و بن ناپدید
شوم غرقه دارم دو یار وفی
همان چشمهٔ شیر و ماء معین
چنین است و این دین و راه منست

It is probably Firdowsi who leans upon a cane at the rail and gazes pensively at the ocean.

Even in a marine subject the artist finds a place for charming wildlife and landscape details.

The court of Gayumars

Gayumars, the first king of Iran, ruled the world from a mountaintop. During his thirty-year reign the arts of life originated: food was discovered and people made clothing of animal skins. Cattle and wild beasts became tame before Gayumars' craggy throne, which men approached with reverence. The king often gazed tearfully upon his son, Siyamak, regretting the day of parting to come. Life was idyllic under Gayumars' just rule until a secret enemy, the div Ahriman, plotted his downfall, aided by the Black Div, his vicious, wolflike son. Although the Iranians were warned by the blessed angel Sorush (standing on a pinnacle near the king), Siyamak was slain in battle against the Black Div.

20

VERSO

This is the miniature by Sultan Muhammad before which, according to Dust Muhammad, his fellow artists hung their heads in shame. It stands as the climax between the traditions of Tabriz under the Turkmans and of Herat under the Timurids. The landscape abounds in concealed grotesques: profoundly tragicomic earth spirits in human and monster forms.

چو آمد ببرج حمل آفتاب
جهان گشت با فر و آیین و آب
بتابید ازان سان ز برج بره
که گیتی جوان شد ازو یکسره
کیومرث چون شد جهان کدخدای
نخستین بکوه اندرون داشت جای
سر تاج و تختش برآمد ز کوه
پلنگینه پوشید خود با گروه
ازو اندر آمد همی پرورش
که پوشیدنی نو بد و نو خورش

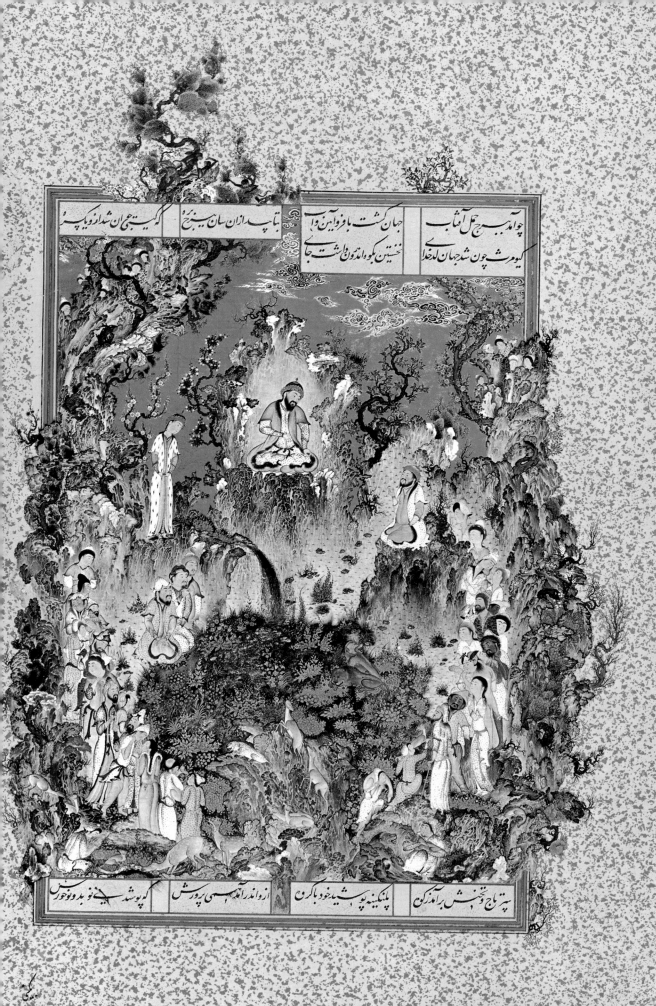

Fated soon to die, Siyamak returns the tender gaze of his father.

Gayumars' people, garbed in pelts, share a blissful existence with the animal kingdom. The ancestors of Sultan Muhammad's lions appear in a Turkman miniature of about 1480 (*see figure* 6).

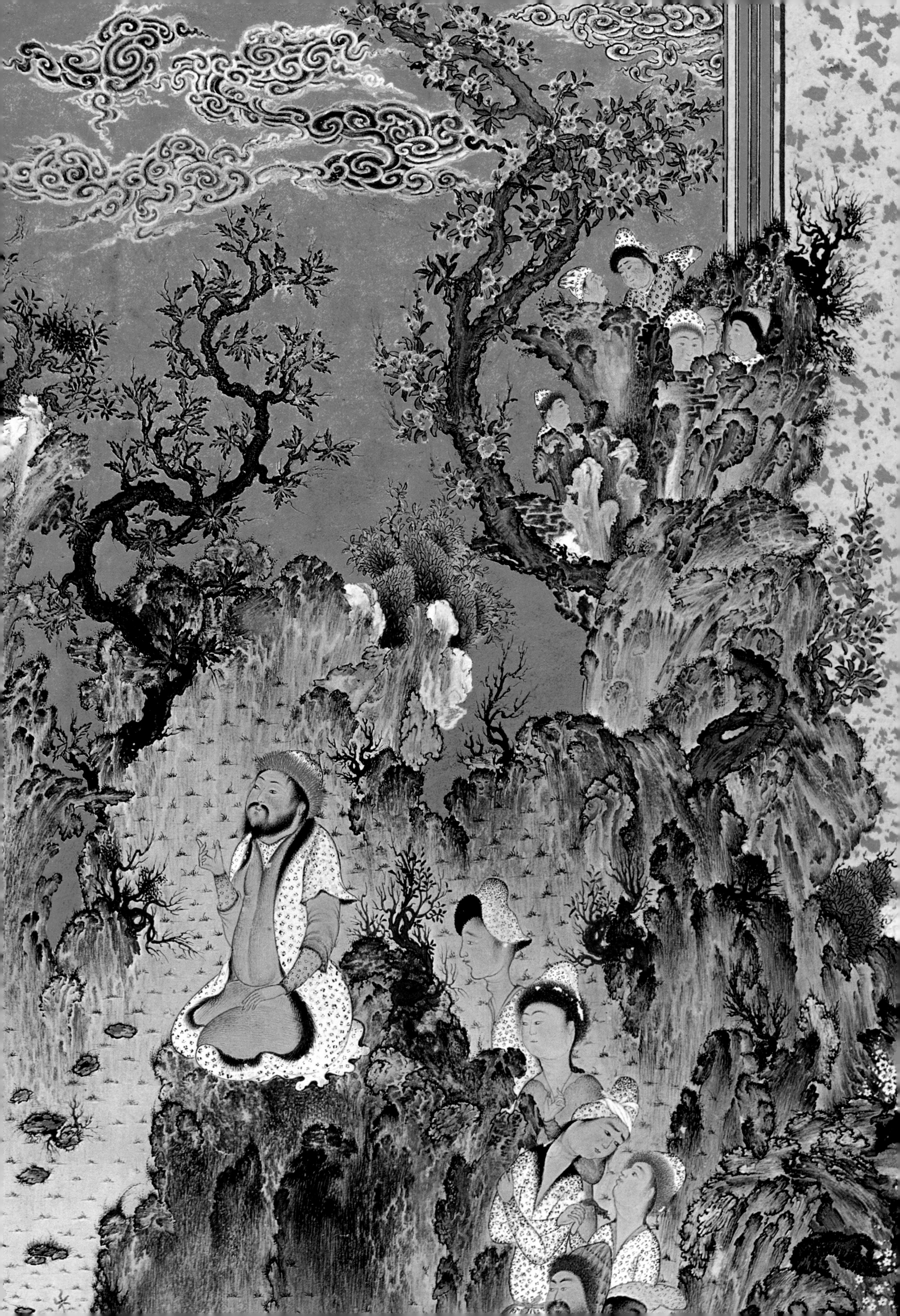

The feast of Sadeh

Gayumars was succeeded by Hushang, the son of Siyamak. Hushang avenged his father's death by slaying the Black Div. During his reign mining, smithery, and animal husbandry were developed. One day Hushang spied a hideous apparition. When he threw a rock at it, the monster vanished. The rock struck a boulder and sparks flashed up. The wise and just Hushang, quick to note the significance of the phenomenon, initiated the worship of fire as a divine gift. That very night he gathered his courtiers and their animals, lectured them about the potentialities of fire, and celebrated the feast known henceforth as Sadeh.

22

VERSO

This is one of Sultan Muhammad's rapidly executed but brilliant illustrations in his variant of the fifteenth-century Turkman style of Tabriz. Though the emphasis is on dash rather than finesse, the witty yet profound characterizations of people and animals make these paintings in the *Shah-nameh* some of his liveliest creations.

بدان ایزدی جاه و فر کیان | ز نخچیر گور و گوزن ژیان | جدا کرد گاو و خر و گوسفند | بورز آورید آنچه بد سودمند

وزیشان بورزید وزیشان چرید | همی خویشتن تاج را پرورید | ز پویندگان هرچه مویش نکوست | بکشت و بسرشان برآهیخت پوست

چو سنجاب و قاقم ز روباه نرم | چهارم سمورست کش موی گرم | برین گونه از چرم پویندگان | بپوشید بالای گویندگان

ببخشید و گسترد و خورد و سپرد | برفت و جز از نام نیکی نبرد | بسی رنج برد اندران روزگار | بافسون و اندیشهٔ بی‌شمار

بگشت از برش بخت سالی چهل | پر از هوش مغز و پر از داد دل | چو پیش آمدش روزگار بهی | ازو مرد را ماند تخت مهی

Again, as in *The court of Gayumars,* Sultan Muhammad has enlivened his rocky landscape with concealed beings from the spirit world.

Sultan Muhammad's animals, painted with sympathy for their inner natures, add up to one of the sprightliest, most comprehensive bestiaries in Islamic art.

Tahmuras defeats the divs

Tahmuras, son of Hushang, carried on his father's good work and improved the techniques of animal husbandry, weaving, and the other arts of life. His greatest deed was the defeat of Ahriman and the divs, whose lives he spared only when they promised to teach him a new and valuable art. This proved to be the alphabet. The demons instructed Tahmuras in a dangerously divisive assortment of tongues and scripts, including Greek, Arabic, Persian, Pahlavi, Soghdian, and Chinese.

23
VERSO

There are Chinese as well as Western influences in this rapidly executed painting by Sultan Muhammad. The flowering plant, upper center, owes its inspiration to the Chinese ornamental blossoms long admired at the Turkman courts, while the foreshortening of several of the horses derives from European art. Again, the artist has peopled his landscape with grotesques. Like many of the miniatures in the first part of the volume, this painting seems closer in spirit to Shah Isma'il than to Prince Tahmasp. One wonders if such paintings and the book itself do not represent an effort on the part of Shah Isma'il and his leading artist to wean the young prince away from his Herat tastes.

جهاندار طهمورث بافرین / بیامد کمربسته رزم و کین
یکایک بیاراست با دیو جنگ / نبد جنگشان را فراوان درنگ

از ایشان دو بهره بافسون ببست / دگرشان بگرز گران کرد پست
کشیدندشان خسته و بسته خوار / بجان خواستند آن زمان زینهار
که ما را مکش تا یکی نو هنر / بیاموزی از ما کت آید ببر
کی نامور دادشان زینهار / بدان تا نهانی کنند آشکار
چو آزاد گشتند از بند اوی / بجستند ناچار پیوند اوی
نبشتن بخسرو بیاموختند / دلش را بدانش بیفروختند
نبشتن یکی نه که نزدیک سی / چه رومی چه تازی و چه پارسی
چه سغدی چه چینی و چه پهلوی / نگاریدن آن کجا بشنوی
جهاندار سی سال ازین بیشتر / تمامی بدید آوریدی هنر
برفت و سرآمد برو روزگار / همه رنج او ماند ازو یادگار

Outfought and humiliated, the divs are ready to negotiate their bad bargain.

Retainers marvel at Tahmuras' handy overthrow of Ahriman and his evil crew.

The nightmare of Zahhak

While yet a prince, Zahhak yielded to the temptation of Iblis (=Ahriman= Satan) and murdered his father, King Mirdas. As a result, two snakes sprouted from his shoulders, snakes that could not be removed and had to be fed on human brains. This horrible development, in conjunction with the tyrant's other crimes, caused his people to rebel. One night, forty years before the end of his reign, Zahhak was visited by a fearful dream of three warriors, one of whom struck him with an ox-head mace. He was then stripped of his skin, from which a rope was twisted to bind him, dust was scattered on his face, and he was dragged past jeering crowds to Mount Damavand. Horrified by this vision, Zahhak awakened with a shriek. The palace shook and the ladies of the harem woke in terror.

28

VERSO

Although the tale is disturbing, its illustrator, Mir Musavvir, the third great senior artist of the book, has depicted a magnificent Safavid palace inhabited by graceful women, pleasing courtiers, and engaging attendants. The color is as subtle as the arabesque patterns on the tiles and textiles. All of this is thoroughly in keeping with the character of Mir Musavvir, the most lyrical of the painters employed on the project. His mellifluous line, calm palette, and gentle approach to people describe a world from which the harsher realities are excluded. Thus, his serpent-ridden tyrant, seen in his bedchamber, is hardly the most interesting figure in the composition.

بجستند خورشید رویان جایی
ازان نامور نعره کدخدای
چنین گفت ضحاک را از نواز
که شاها چه بودت نگویی براز

Men of the palace, one of them comically losing his turban, react to the shriek of horror in the royal chamber.

Finger to mouth, ladies of the palace register astonishment at the nocturnal alarm.

Zahhak is told his fate

Next day, the tyrant called together the magi, astrologers, and other wise men of his realm to expound his dream. Though he commanded the assembly to prophesy or suffer death, only honest Zirak dared speak out. He predicted that Faridun, a warrior not yet born, would carry out the horrors Zahhak had known in his sleep. Zahhak would be struck down with an ox-head mace and dragged through the streets in bonds to avenge deeds that he had yet to perpetrate: the execution of Faridun's father and the slaying of the cow Birmayeh. Hearing this, the tyrant swooned. Zirak, fearful of his life for speaking the truth, fled.

29
VERSO

By Sultan Muhammad, this painting reveals the strong impact of Bihzad, the Timurid master who probably came to Tabriz as part of Prince Tahmasp's entourage. The logically arranged architecture and people, the minutely brushed, small-scale figures, the naturalistic characterizations, and the restrained palette are all the work of the brilliant Tabriz artist striving to beat the Herat master at his own game.

زند بر سرت گرزهٔ گاو روی   ببندت وارد ز ایوان بکوی
دلاور بدو گفت اگر بخردی   کسی بی بهانه نیازردی
یکی گاو برمایه خواهد بدن   جهانجوی را دایه خواهد بدن
چو ضحاک بشنید بگشاد گوش   ز تخت اندر افتاد و زو رفت هوش
بدو گفت ضحاک ناپاک دین   چرا بندد م بانیش بی کین
برآید بدست تو هوش پدرش   وزان درد گردد پر از کینه سرش
تبه گردد آن هم بدست تو بر   بدین کین کشد گرزهٔ گاو سر

گرانمایه از پیش تخت بلند   بتا پدر رویش ز بیم گزند
نشان فریدون بگرد جهان   همی باز جست آشکار و نهان
چو آمد دل تاجور باز جای   بتخت کیان اندر آورد پای
نه آرام بودش نه خواب و نه خورد   شده روز روشن برو لاجورد
برآمد برین روزگار دراز   کشید اژدهافش بتنگی فراز
خجسته فریدون ز مادر بزاد   جهان را یکی دیگر آمد نهاد

زادن فریدون از مادر و
داستان گاوی که او را دایه بود

Sultan Muhammad's vigorous arabesque ornament, which, like his figure painting, owes much to the Tabriz tradition, is here incorporated into a classically balanced whole.

The figures at the fence (right) are painted with the same earthy humor and sketchiness found in *Tahmuras defeats the divs.* Save for such unmistakable indications, one might assign this painting to Bihzad himself.

Zahhak slays Birmayeh

Zirak's dreadful predictions came to pass. Faridun was born. Abtin, his father, was captured and executed at Zahhak's command. Faridun's mother, the wise Faranak, fled with her son and gave him over to a peasant who fed him with milk from the extraordinary cow-nurse, Birmayeh. News of the peacock-hued cow reached Zahhak, who rushed to the scene like a mad elephant, slew her, and burned Faridun's palace to the ground. But Faranak, having sensed the danger, had already escaped with Faridun.

30

VERSO

Also by Sultan Muhammad, this miniature contains one of his most beautiful trees, a particularly poetic plane with elegantly pointed leaves and white branches that reach out with the vitality of dragons.

خبر شد بضحاک یک روزگار
ازان گاو پرمایه و مرغزار
بیامد پر از کینه چون پیل مست
مران گاو پرمایه را کرد پست
همی هرچه دید اندرو چارپای
بیفگند وزیشان بپرداخت جای
سبک سوی خان فریدون شتافت
فراوان پژوهید و کس را نیافت
بایوان او آتش اندر فگند
ز پای اندر آورد کاخ بلند
چو بگذشت بر آفریدون دو هشت
ز البرز کوه اندر آمد بدشت
بر مادر آمد پژوهید و گفت
که بگشای بر من نهان از نهفت
بگو مر مرا تا که بودم پدر
کیم من ز تخم از کدامین گهر
پرسیدن فریدون نژاد خود را از مادر

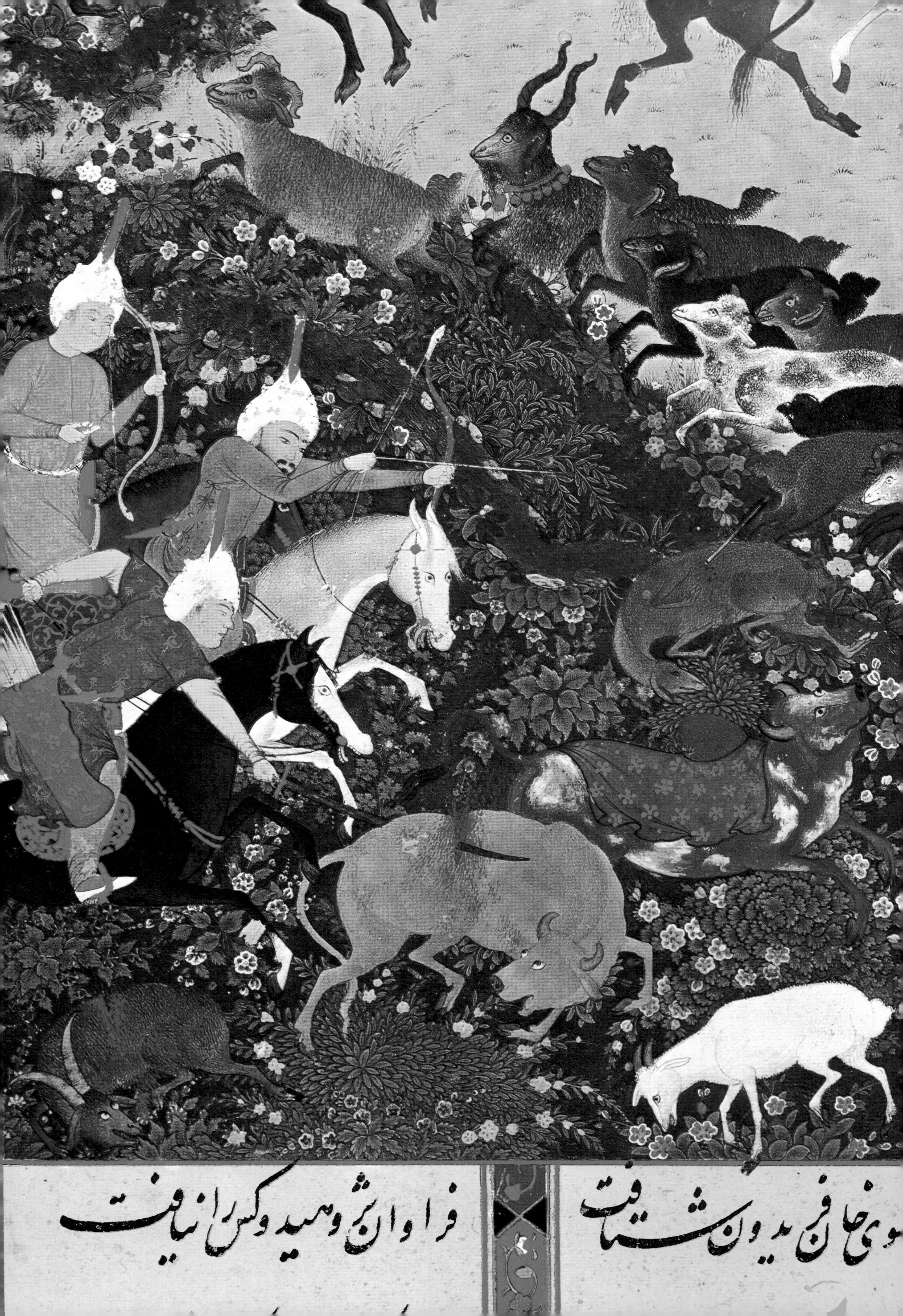
خان فریدون شتافت
کس را نیافت

While the tyrant (above) commits one of the terrible deeds foretold by Zirak, his followers wantonly destroy Faridun's herds.

Faridun strikes down Zahhak

Grown to manhood, Faridun led a vigorous campaign against Zahhak. In time, he enthroned himself in the tyrant's palace at Dizh-hukht Gang and liberated the daughters of King Jamshid, whose minds he found addled by Zahhak's wickedness. Climbing the palace battlement and spying Faridun in the throne room with his erstwhile favorites, the maddened Zahhak lowered himself through a window and charged, scimitar in hand, whereupon the young hero struck him down with his ox-head mace. As Faridun prepared to finish the villain the angel Sorush swooped down and stayed his hand. "Zahhak's time has not yet come," he warned. "Bind him tightly and take him to some gorge where his followers cannot find him."

36

VERSO

When this picture was painted, Sultan Muhammad was at home in the new mode, a synthesis of the traditions of Tabriz and Herat. Here he has created a dramatic composition in which the blow of Faridun's mace is accentuated by the "weight" of the architecture, the mass of the gold throne, and even by the placement of the angel, whose sinuous lines set up a rhythm that can be traced all the way to the tyrant's head.

همیدون بکنگ بسته بندش چو سنگ
بیر تا دو کوه آیدت پیش تنگ
بکوه اندرون بود بنداوی
نیامد برش خویش و پیوند اوی
فریدون چو بشنید ناسود دیر
کمندی برآراست از چرم شیر

بران پیشش

Sorush intervenes, saving Zahhak for the end foretold by Zirak.

One of Jamshid's daughters looks on, amazed as her oppressor is laid low.

The death of Zahhak

The tyrant was carried in chains toward Shirkhan, where Faridun proposed to cast him from the mountaintop. But Sorush whispered to Faridun that, instead, the captive should be chained alive at the summit of Mount Damavand, the greatest peak in Iran, so that his brain might chafe and his agony endure. Faridun chose a narrow gorge for the dragon king and his snakes, and there he was left.

37
VERSO

While *The court of Gayumars* is the masterpiece of the early years of the *Shahnameh* project, this picture, also by Sultan Muhammad, is his greatest painting in the manner of the later 1530s. It is in the infinitely detailed and more naturalistic mode of the British Museum's *Khamseh* of Nizami of 1539 to 43 (page 63). The less important faces in our painting seem to have been done by one of the younger artists, Mir Sayyid Ali.

فروبست دستش بر آن کوه باز
بدان تا بماند بسختی دراز
بماند او برین گونه آویخته
وزو خون دل بر زمین ریخته
بیا تا جهانرا ببد نسپریم
بکوشش همه دست نیکی بریم
نباشد همی نیک و بد پایدار
همان به که نیکی بود یادگار
سخن ماند از تو همی یادگار
سخن را چنین خوار مایه مدار

The dragons in these clouds hark back to the Turkman style of Tabriz. In contrast, the countenances in the rocks have become so naturalistic they bring to mind eighteenth-century English portraiture.

Even at this climactic moment there is a place for lute music beside an inviting stream.

Faridun tests his sons

Upon the death of Zahhak, Faridun reigned supreme, dispensing justice by binding evil hands with kindness. Mankind turned once again to God, and the world became a paradise. After fifty years Faridun had three sons, tall as cypresses, swift and powerful as elephants, and with cheeks like spring. In his love for them Faridun refused to tempt fate by assigning them names. When they came of marriageable age, he sought them suitable wives. Through the services of an emissary, he discovered three pearl-like princesses, daughters of King Sarv of Yemen. The nameless sons journeyed to Yemen, married the girls, and brought them home.

They were met by a dragon: Faridun in disguise. Scattering dust clouds and bellowing, Faridun charged his eldest son, who retreated in terror, remarking that no sensible man fights dragons. Faridun then turned upon his second son, who drew his bow threateningly and boasted that it made no difference whether he fought a raging lion or a cavalier. The youngest son, confronted next, cried, "Be off! You are a mere crocodile; beware of lions! If you have heard of Faridun, you will not dare fight us, for we are his sons and each of us is a warrior like him."

At the palace, Faridun met his sons in human form and at last gave them names. The eldest, who had prudently sought safety, he called Salm. The second, whose courage was more ardent than flame, was named Tur. The youngest, who had chosen the middle course, he named Iraj.

Reading his sons' horoscopes and learning that Iraj, his favorite, had been born with a woeful destiny, Faridun sought to avoid tragedy by dividing his kingdom. Rum (Byzantium) and all the West were made Salm's, and he was sent off with an army to his domain. Turan and Chin (Central Asia and all the East) were given to Tur. Iran and the special honors due the first kingdom of the world were given to Iraj. Thus was the stage set for one of the major themes of the *Shahnameh,* the rivalry among the kingdoms.

All too soon the guileless Iraj was lured abroad and done to death by his envious brothers. Damning the murderers, Faridun asked of God that he live only long enough to see vengeance done by someone of the seed of Iraj. In time his prayer was answered: Manuchihr, the cherished grandson of Iraj, delivered the wicked heads of Tur and Salm.

42

VERSO

This is one of the finest miniatures in the book attributable to Aqa Mirak. It must have been painted toward the end of the 1530s, since the style is that of the British Museum's *Khamseh* miniatures of 1539–43. Many details of the handling, including the sinuously organic composition, the vitreous rocks with their concealed forms, and the specific characterizations of people and animals support the attribution to Aqa Mirak.

خروشان و جوشان بجنبش درون
برانگیخت گرد و برآورد جوش
بمهتر گفت با اژدها روز جنگ
میانه برادر چو او را بدید
همی خواست با او نبرد آورد
بدو گفت کز پیش ما دور شو
گرت نام شاه آفریدون بگوش
که فرزند اوییم هر سه پسر
همی از دهانش آمد آتش برون
جهان گشت از آوای او پر خروش
بنیارد خرد یافته مرد سنگ
سبک تیغ تیز از میان برکشید
پس اژدها را بگرد آورد
چو هر سه پسر را بنزدیک دید
بیامد دمان سوی مهتر پسر
سبک پشت بنمود و بگریخت زو
بدل گفت اگر کارزار است کار
چو کهتر پسر نزد ایشان رسید
بگرد اندرون کوه تاریک دید
که او بود پرمایه و تاجور
پدر زی برادرش بنهاد روی
چو شیر دمنده چو جنگی سوار
خروشید کان اژدها را بد
نهنگی تو بر راه شیران مرو
رسیدست با ما بدینسان مکوش
همه گرزداران پرخاشخر
گر از راه بیراه یکسو شوی
فریدون فرخ چو بشنید وی
رها جانت از تیره خسروی
سخنها بدیشان شد ناپدید

پر اژدها را بگرد آورد
چو کهتر پسر نزد ایشان رسید
خروشید کان اژدها را بد
نهنگی تو بر راه شیران مرو
رسیدست با ما بدینسان مکوش
همه گرز داران پرخاشخر

Aqa Mirak's dragon is one of the liveliest, his bear one of the most delightful, in Safavid art.

Sam comes to Mount Alburz

Sam, the paladin in whose care Faridun had put the infant Manuchihr, grandson of the murdered Iraj, was sorely troubled at not having an heir of his own. Happily, one of his wives at last became pregnant. But when the child was born, he suffered from a fearful blemish: his hair was white. Sam asked forgiveness of heaven for whatever offense deserved such shame, and, though he admired the infant, he had him carried away and exposed upon Mount Alburz. For a day and a night the boy lay wailing where he had been cast. Then the simurgh, the miraculous bird that dwelt upon the mount, took him up in her claws and carried him to the peak. Here, at the behest of God, she fed and protected him along with her own young.

After a time, passing caravans saw a noble young man, his chest a mountain of silver, his waist a reed, in the bird's nest. Rumor of this remarkable presence finally reached Sam, who was encouraged by his wise men to hasten to the scene. There, looking up, he saw his son, but when he tried to climb toward him, he could find no way to the lofty perch. He then prayed to God, asking forgiveness and help. A moment later the simurgh saw Sam and knew that he had come for her charge. The devoted bird gave the youth a plume. "Burn this if ever you have need of me," she said. "And may your heart never forget your nurse, whose heart breaks for love of you."

63

VERSO This brilliantly designed page can be assigned to Painter D, one of Sultan Muhammad's assistants. Although it was wholly painted by him, and its rocks are inhabited with his particular sort of grotesque, the inspiration for the picture, with its soaring cliffs, was Sultan Muhammad's *Court of Gayumars*.

نپشته چو لی بکردار سام
بدیدش که می گشت گرد کنام
بدانست کو دادگر داور است
توانا و بر برتران برتر است
ره بر شدن جست و کی بود راه
دد و دام را بر جنان جایگاه
همی گفت کای برتر از جایگاه
ز روشن گمان و ز خورشید و ماه
بپوزش بر تو پیر افکنده ام
ز بر ترس تو جانرا پر کنده ام
ازین بر شدن بنده را دستگیر
مر این پر گنه را تو کن دلپذیر
گر این کودک از پاک پشت منست
نه از تخم بدگوهر آهرمنست
برحمت برافراز این بنده را
بمن باز ده پور افکنده را
چو باد آور این راز ناگفته شد
ستایش همانا که بدرفته شد

The simurgh's rich plumage recalls Turkman drawings intended as guides for embroiderers.

Moplike trees that flip-flop in arabesque rhythms are typical of Painter D.

Zal receives Mihrab's homage at Kabul

Sam named his son Zal ("The Old"), in allusion to his white hair, and made every effort to redress past wrongs. Manuchihr, too, gave the young man due regard. When Sam went off to wage war in Mazandaran, Zal, recommended to the elders, was given Sam's kingdom. Zal's rule was auspicious, his wisdom great. People thronged to behold him, amazed at his beauty. His camphor-white locks now seemed dark and beautiful as musk. Setting forth on a royal progress to view his eastern provinces, Zal at every stage held court and called for wine, harp, and minstrelsy. In Kabul, Mihrab, a vassal king descended from the evil Zahhak, paid homage with gifts of horses, slaves, coins, brocades, musk, and a jeweled crown.

67

VERSO This sunlit reception scene, with its atmosphere of a garden party, can be assigned to Mir Musavvir, who has peopled it with his usual cast of handsome and amiable courtiers.

ز زابل بکابل رسید آنزمان
گرازان و خندان و دل شادمان
یکی پادشا بود مهراب نام
زبردست و با گنج و گسترده کام
ببالا بکردار آزاد سرو
برخ چون بهار و برفتن تذرو
دل بخردان داشت و مغز ردان
دو کتف یلان و هش موبدان
ز ضحاک تازی گهر داشتی
بکابل همه بوم و بر داشتی
همیداد هر سال با سام ساو
چو آگه شد از کار دستان سام
ز کابل بیامد بهنگام بام
ابا گنج و اسپان آراسته
غلامان و هرگونه خواسته
ز دینار و یاقوت و مشک و عبیر
ز دیبای زربفت و خز و حریر
یکی تاج پرگوهر شاهوار
یکی طوق زرین زبرجد نگار
بیاورد با خویشتن سوی راه
چو آمد بدستان سام آگهی

یکی پادشا بود مهراب نام
زبردست و با گنج و گسترده کام
دل بخردان داشت و مغز ردان
دو کتف یلان و هش موبدان
همی داد هر سال ما سام ساو
ابا گنج و اسپان آراسته
غلامان و هرگونه خواسته

Mir Musavvir's dwarf, standing near Zal, pleases the eye with his well-rounded form.

Mihrab wears his humility easily as his train of gifts passes. The rotund courtier at the upper right may be another portrait of Karpuz Sultan (*see figure 14*).

Zal consults the magi

Learning of Rudabeh, Mihrab's beautiful daughter, Zal lost his heart in love. But the affair was to progress slowly. Zal rightly feared that his father and Manuchihr would disapprove his marrying a descendant of Zahhak, and while Mihrab generally approved of the young prince, some of Zal's actions made him bristle. For her part, Rudabeh loved Zal as much as he loved her. Here we witness the troubled Zal asking the advice of his wise men.

73
VERSO

This miniature is the result of a happy collaboration between Sultan Muhammad and Painter D, his assistant. Sultan Muhammad would seem to have designed the picture and painted several portions of it, notably the figure in the foreground and the youths to the left of the throne. The rest of the work is largely D's.

زبان تیز بگشاد و پیش ان سلام
چنین گفت کز داور پاک داد
بخشایش اندر بترس از گناه
خداوند گردنده خورشید و ماه
بهار آرد و تیر ماه و خزان
لبی پر ز خنده دلی شاد کام
روا از به سینگی نماینده راه
برارد نو میوه دار از رزان
نخست آفرین بر جهاندار کرد
بدو نیست کیهان خرم بپای
دل موبد از خواب بیدار کرد
دل ما پر از ترس و امید باد
بفرمانها ژرف کردن نگاه
نمود او داور و رهبر دو سرای
جوان دارد ش کاه بارنگ و بوی
ز فرمان و رایش کسی نگذرد
کهش پر ببینی ز شرم کرده روی
پی مور بینی او زمین نسپرد

The wise men propose that Zal write a letter to his father. "He has greater wisdom than we have," they counsel. "Perhaps he will intercede with the shah."

Instilled with the master's humor and psychological insight, this abashed figure was surely painted by Sultan Muhammad.

Qaran slays Barman

The death of the old shah, Manuchihr, and of the old paladin, Sam, ended the period of Iranian supremacy. The unity of the great age of Faridun had been destroyed by the vendetta begun with the slaying of Iraj. The Iranian side had been avenged when Manuchihr killed Tur and Salm. It was now once again the turn of the Turanians, whose shah was Pashang. The Turanians' great paladin was Afrasiyab, Pashang's son. Burning to take vengeance upon the weakened houses of Manuchihr and Sam, Afrasiyab led a huge army across the Oxus River boundary. Shah Nowzar, Manuchihr's son, headed the Iranian force and met the invasion. The first engagement ended in a stalemate. Barman, the fiery young nephew of the Turanian ruler, persuaded his uncle to let him engage one of the enemy in individual combat. Qaran, the Iranian commander, looked about for a volunteer, but only old Qubad, his own brother, responded. The Turanian and the Iranian fought from dawn till dusk. When the lion-hearted old man, pierced by Barman's lance, fell headlong from his horse, the war began in earnest. After the Turanians had won three battles, Barman, slayer of Qubad, was slain by Qaran with the same lance-stroke that killed his brother. In the sequel, Shah Nowzar was captured and bound in Turanian chains.

102

VERSO

This battle scene, with its eerie nocturnal palette, is the last picture in the sequence of the manuscript that can be assigned to Sultan Muhammad, and it would seem that he was assisted in coloring it by a younger artist, Mir Sayyid Ali, one of the masters of the second generation. The hand of the younger man is evident in the treatment of many of the faces, also in the treatment of some of the horses and their trappings. While Sultan Muhammad invariably gave his characters life, the younger man, who was a brilliant designer and an almost miraculously fine craftsman, painted people and animals as still life. Later, Mir Sayyid Ali went to India and became one of the founders of the Mughal school of painting.

از و قارن رزم زن خسته بود
بخون برادر کمر بسته بود
برآویخت چون شیر با بارمان
سوی چاره جستن نبودش امان
یکی نیزه زد بر کمربند او
که بگسست بنیاد و پیوند او
فرود آمد و سر بریدش ز تن
برآویخت از زین کوه انجمن
بفرمود قارن بیاران خود
که ای نامداران و گردان د
برآید ازین نابکاران دمار
که برگشته بختند و بد روزگار
بکشتند چندی ز توران سپاه
به بستند دیگر بسی کینه خواه
برفتند نزدیک افراسیاب
غمین گشته از رزم و دل پرشتاب
وز آنسو که بد شاه نوذر بجای
در اندیشه بد تا چه آرد خدای
چو آگاه شد نامور پادشاه
که قارن گذر کرد از آن رزمگاه
غمی گشت و لشکر همه برگرفت
چو تیر از پس روی بنهاد و رفت
همی خواست کز روز بد بگذرد
سپهرش مگر زیر پی بسترد
چنین گفت روشن دلی تیزهوش
پسزد گر گشاسپی به پند گوش
ز تقدیر کس نگذرد بیگمان
اگر خود بپرد بسوی آسمان
چنین است گردون ناپایدار
که با کس نباشد همی سازگار
اگر شهریارست اگر گله بان
چو روزش سرآمد نبخشد امان
چو افراسیاب آگهی یافت زو
که سوی بیابان نهان کرد رو
سپاه انجمن کرد و پویان برفت
دمان از پس شاه جویان برفت

Drums thunder and trumpets blare as the Iranian and Turanian armies clash.

Three Turanians are driven from the field. Their dress, like the Iranians', is up to date: they wear the headgear of the Safavids' contemporary enemy, the Ottoman Turks.

گرفتار گشتن نه والا بود | نشیبست جایی که بالا بود
پسر و گر نیاری بایشان گزند | بمنشان سپاری همیدون به بند
بایشان یکی خانه زندان کنم | نگهدارشان هوشمندان کنم
بسپاری بزاری برآرند هوش | تو از خون کشش دست و چندین مکوش
چو کشتی شهنشاشان بیگناه | نه زیبد که لشکر بسازی تباه
کنون بند بهتر ایا تاجور | مبادا پشیمانی آید ببر
چو بشنید گفتار او تاجور | نه پیچید از رای آن نامور
بفرمودشان تا بساری برند | بمسمار و غل و بخواری برند
بدین کار اغریرث آمد به پیش | نگهبان گردان ها گیره کیش
ببردند از پیش افراسیاب | مر آن نامداران پر از پیچ و تاب
چو این کرده شد ساز رفتن گرفت | جهان زیر اسپان نهفتن گرفت
به پیش دهستان ری در کشید | از ایشان برنج و تنگ خوی کشید
از آن پس بیامد بایران زمین | جهانی در آورد زیر نگین
کلاه کیانی بسر بر نهاد | بدینار دادن در اندر گشاد

Afrasiyab on the Iranian throne

When Zal slew Khazarvan, a Turanian leader, in battle and sent a new Turanian army bolting like sheep in a storm, Afrasiyab's heart was pained. "My friends are vilely slaughtered even though Nowzar is my prisoner. Bring me the shah," he bellowed, "that I may teach him war!" Declaring that Nowzar, inheritor of the ancestral feud from the time of Salm and Tur, deserved his fate, Afrasiyab called for his scimitar, sliced off the shah's head, and had his body flung in the dust. Afrasiyab then marched from Dahistan to Ray, where he assumed the crown of Iran.

105

RECTO

By Painter E, one of the lesser hands of the project, this miniature is typical of the artist's old-fashioned, stiff style. Certainly he was a dedicated and accomplished craftsman, and his ornamentation is excellent. Yet his characterizations lack the vitality that is so evident in the work, say, of Sultan Muhammad. E's faces are generally alike, with eyes that too often seem blankly unfocused.

Having brought the world under his signet ring, Afrasiyab, enthroned beneath an opulent canopy, begins distributing the gold of Iran.

The usurper's minions parcel out Iranian treasure.

Rustam finds Kay Qubad

Zal gathered an army to drive Afrasiyab from Iran, but there was no shah to lead it. Then one of the magi told Zal of Kay Qubad, a descendant of Faridun, in whom grace, modesty, and legal claim were combined. While the army waited, the hero Rustam, son of Zal and Rudabeh, was sent in search of the future king and founder of the Kayanian dynasty. Within a mile of Mount Alburz, Rustam came upon a garden spot of streams, flowers, and trees. Here, on a throne sprinkled with rose water and musk, sat a young man resembling the moon, attended by a court of noblemen. The noblemen came forward to greet Rustam, entreating him to dismount so they might drink his health. Not knowing whom he had encountered, Rustam was reluctant to delay his quest, but he was led to the throne. The moon-like youth took his hand and drank a toast: "To the free." He then revealed that he was Kay Qubad. Further toasts were drunk, after which the two rode off to the waiting throne of Iran.

110

VERSO

This brightly colored miniature can be assigned to Aqa Mirak, who created a similarly designed and colored picture a decade or so later for the British Museum's *Khamseh* of 1539–43. Here he is painting in a somewhat simplified style, comparable to the sketchier work for the project by Sultan Muhammad.

بگویی که گردان ترا خواستند
بشادی جهان پیاراستند
زگفتار رستم دلیر جوان
بخندید وگفتش که ای پهلوان
زتخم فریدون منم کیقباد
پدر بر پدر نام دارم بیاد
نشان ازتوانی ودانی ورا
دهی وبشاهی برپانی ورا
چو بشنید رستم فرو برد سر
بخدمت فرود آمد ازتخت زر

While musicians play (left), Rustam is made welcome. On the shoulder of his tiger-skin robe is a yang and yin symbol, a motif the artist also painted in the British Museum's *Khamseh* of Nizami. Kay Qubad's followers (above), represented in the guise of Shah Tahmasp's courtiers, enjoy life al fresco.

Rustam's fourth course: he cleaves a witch

Following the Iranians' rout of Afrasiyab, Kay Qubad ruled Iran for a hundred years. He was succeeded by his eldest son, Kay Kavus, who, alas, abandoned the path of wisdom. In his vanity and pride, he overrode the stern admonitions of Zal and led an expedition into Mazandaran, a province notorious for its divs. At first the campaign was a success, but then the div king called upon his ally, the White Div, who spread a blinding cloud upon the Iranian host. Hemmed in by an army of twelve thousand demons, Kay Kavus regretted his rejection of Zal's wise counsel and sent a warrior to Zal and to Rustam blaming himself for the disastrous happenings and entreating help.

Undertaking the rescue mission with some reluctance, Rustam headed for Mazandaran by a short and dangerous route, a gloomy road haunted by divs and lions. One of his challenges, known as a course, took place when Rustam and his horse Rakhsh reached an inviting site beside a stream and beheld there a roasted sheep, bread, spices, sweetmeats, wine, and a lute. Reminded of God's previous blessings to him, Rustam dismounted, partook of the wine, picked up the lute, and improvised a song about his life—one perpetual engagement with dragon, div, and desert. His singing attracted one of the party of witches whose repast he had interrupted. She took on the guise of a moon-faced girl, scented with musk and decked out in beautiful colors. Not knowing that she was really Ahriman (the devil), Rustam saw her as yet another of God's bounties and invited her to join him in a cup of wine. He soon found her out: when he thanked God for his generosity the girl's aspect changed. Far from joining in his prayer, she turned black. Quick as the wind, Rustam caught her in his lasso, whereupon she became a fetid hag, all guile and wrinkle. Rustam forthwith sliced her through with his scimitar.

120

VERSO By Painter A, this picture owes much to the demons of the Turkman albums (page 41).

بینداخت از باد خم کمند | برازرنگ و نیرنگ بندو گرند | میانش بخنجر بدو نیم کرد | دل جادوان زو پر از بیم کرد

وزانجا سوی راه بنهاد روی | چنان چون بود مردم راه‌جوی | همی رفت پویان بجایی رسید | که اندر جهان روشنایی ندید

شب تیره چون روی زنگی سیاه | ستاره نه پیدا نه تابنده ماه | تو خورشید گفتی سد اندرست | ستاره بخم کمند اندرست

عنان رخش را داد و بنهاد روی | نه افراز دید از سیاهی نه جوی | وزانجا سوی روشنایی رسید | زمین پرنیان یکسر خوید

جهانی ز پیری شده نوجوان | همه سبزه و آبهای روان | همه جامه برتنش چون آب بود | نیازش باسایش و خواب بود

Two of the divs are astounded and dismayed by the violent end of their associate.

With Rakhsh noisily urging him on, Rustam pays the witch for her treachery.

The shah's war prizes are pledged for

Kay Khosrow, the son of Siyavush, a tragically slain hero, became shah on the abdication of his grandfather, the prideful Kay Kavus. In due course Kay Khosrow's mind turned to the villainy of Afrasiyab, and he prepared for war. At a gathering of the warriors of Iran he offered jewels, gold coin, and a hundred pieces of rich brocade to the hero who would bring him the vile head of Palashan, Afrasiyab's commander-in-chief. Bizhan, son of Giv, volunteered instantly. The shah then indicated a wealth of embroideries, furs, and a pair of rosy-cheeked slaves. "I will confer these and still more favors," he declared, "to the man who brings me the crown of Tazhav, Afrasiyab's son-in-law." Again Bizhan arose, to the wonderment of those assembled. Ten slave boys, ten steeds with golden bridles, and ten veiled maidens were next offered to the paladin who would capture for the shah Tazhav's heart-alluring concubine, Ispanuy. Bizhan volunteered a third time. The fourth offer of the shah was accepted by Bizhan's father, Giv. In return for seven jeweled cups filled with precious stones and scents, ten slaves, and ten horses, Giv pledged to deliver Tazhav's head. The fifth offer, likewise accepted by Giv, was the most lavish of all: musk and jewels, ten golden trays laden with dinars, ten peri-faced slaves with fitting headgear and belts, and two hundred pieces of silk and gold brocade. For this prize Giv volunteered to set afire the barricade of logs that the Turanians had built mountain high at a strategic crossing point on the river Kaseh.

225

VERSO This is another simplified painting by Aqa Mirak, whose immaculate perfection of color, subtle sense of balance, and purity of outline make it a particularly striking composition. Many of this artist's miniatures in the *Shah-nameh* are in this mode.

وزان پس بگنجور فرمود شاه
که ده خوان زرین بنه پیشگاه
دو صد خنجر و پای بی کیر بر
یکی خسروی افسر و ده کمر
بر و برز دینار و مشک و گهر
پری روی ده با کلاه و کمر
از ایدر شوم تا سوی کاسه رود
دمم بر روان سیاوش درود
سپهدار سالار توران سپاه
برآورد آن کوه هیزم براه
که نامد خبر نزد کاوس شاه
ز کار سیاوش که گشت او تباه
دلیری ز ایران بباید شدن
همه کاسه رود آتش اندر زدن
بشه گیو گفت این گه رزم نیست
برافروختن کوه کار منست
چنین گفت کین هیمه آنرا کبرخ
ندارد دریغ از پی تاج و گنج
ز هیزم یکی کوه بینید بلند
فزونست بالاش از صد کمند
چنان خواست کان راه کس نسپرد
از ایران بتوران کسی نگذرد
ز هیزم فروبست آن راه را
چو دریغ کرد اختر شاه را
بدان تا گر آنجا بود رزمگاه
پس هیزم اندر بماند سپاه
همه مرز را آتش اندر زنم
بنیزه که از جای من بکنم

Kay Khosrow accepts Bizhan's pledges.

Trays of jewels are brought forth.

یکی جنگ باپشن افکند پی
که این دشت جنگست یا جای می
سپاه اندر آمد بگرد سپاه
یکی بانگ برخاست از رزمگاه
سراسیمه شد مست از دار و گیر
برآمد یکی ابر بار آتش تیر
بزیر سر مست بالین نرم
ز بر تیغ و شمشیر و کوپال گرم
سپیده چو برزد سر از برج شیر
بلشکر نگه کرد گیو دلیر
همه دشت از ایرانیان کشته دید
ز لشکر دلیران و مردان بد
همه رزمگه سربسر کشته دید
زمین سربسر چون گل آغشته دید
دریده درفش و نگون کرده کوس
رخ زندگان گشته چون آبنوس
همی کرد گودرز هر سو نگاه
ز دشمن نفیر و دم سپاه
بدان اندکی برکشیدند نخ
سپاهی ز زنگان چو مور و ملخ
پدر بی پسر شد پسر بی پدر
همه لشکرش زیر و زبر
چنین آمد این گنبد تیز گرد
گهی شادمانی دهد گاه درد

The besotted Iranian camp attacked

The fortunes of war brought each side its share of victories and defeats. When the Iranians had successfully advanced, Afrasiyab berated Piran, his aged commander, who thereupon gathered an enormous army and led it toward the Iranian camp. According to the Turanian spies, the Iranians, led by Tus, held back. "Instead of war drums," the spies reported, "we hear the sound of merriment and drinking." Furthermore, it appeared that the overconfident Iranians had posted no guards. Piran chose thirty thousand horsemen and in the dead of night charged without warning. Giv, hearing the clamor of enemy arms, managed to stagger to his horse. Raging like a leopard at his own stupor, he tried to rouse the camp to resistance. To no avail: hot Turanian swords, scimitars, and maces played freely over Iranian heads lolling on the soft cushions of revelry. By morning the plain was covered with Iranian blood, flags were torn, kettle-drums were overturned, and the survivors' cheeks were like ebony. Two thirds of the once proud Iranian army had been wiped out.

241

RECTO

Painter A has here created one of his most successful and high-spirited miniatures, a tragicomic scene in which he pokes hearty fun at the shortcomings of the military. If we look closely, the faces appear to be caricatures of universal military types.

Unequal combat in the night.

Beset, an Iranian deflects a spear.

برون شد بنخچیر چون نره شیر
کمندی بدست اژدهای بزیر
سه روزش همی جست از آن مرغزار
همی کرد برگرد اسپان شکار
درخشنده زرین یکی باره بود
بچرم اندرون زشت بتیاره بود
چنین گفت کین را نباید فکند
ببایدگرفتن بخم کمند
بدشتی کجا داشت چوبان گله
بدانجا گذر داشت گور یله
چهارم بدیدش گرازان بدشت
چو باد شمالی برو برگذشت
برانگیخت رستم تگاور ز جای
چو شنگ اندر آمد دگر شد برای
نبایدش کردن بنخجیر تباه
برینسانش زنده برم نزد شاه
بینداخت رستم کیانی کمند
همی خواست کاردسرش را ببند

Rustam pursues Akvan

One day a herdsman sought Kay Khosrow's assistance against a ferocious div in the form of an onager who attacked horses. The shah, sensing that only a lionlike champion would do, summoned his warriors but found none to please him. Only Rustam, son of Zal, could help. For three days Rustam searched the countryside without luck. On the fourth day an onager rushed past him like the north wind. The hero spurred Rakhsh, thinking that he would capture this animal and lead it before the shah. When the onager sighted Rustam's noose and vanished instantly, Rustam knew that he was pursuing no ordinary onager but the div Akvan himself in disguise. After further monumental hazards and reverses Rustam slew the animal with his sword and carried his head to Kay Khosrow.

294

RECTO This is an early work by Muzaffar Ali, a contemporary of Shah Tahmasp. Later, Muzaffar Ali contributed to the British Museum's *Khamseh* of Nizami and to the 1556–65 *Haft Awrang* of Jami (page 67).

Turmoil among the horses as Akvan evades capture.

Rustam hopes to take the onager alive.

The first joust of the rooks: Fariburz versus Kalbad

After a deadlock between the armies of Iran and Turan, the two commanders-in-chief, Gudarz and Piran, met and agreed to avoid further useless carnage. Instead, they would personally engage in single combat, and each would furthermore choose ten of his valiant men (rooks) who would likewise joust individually. The duels would be fought between two hills, one for Turan, the other for Iran, and each victor would plant his flag on the appropriate hill to proclaim his success. Fariburz, son of Shah Kay Kavus, was the first to take the field. His opponent was Kalbad, a brother of the Turanian commander. Though his arrows missed their mark, Fariburz found time to draw his glittering sword and cleave his foe from neck to waist.

341

VERSO One of a series in archaic style, illustrating *The joust of the eleven rooks,* this miniature can be attributed to Shaykh Muhammad, a younger artist who frequently worked with Dust Muhammad. He has derived the poses of his horsemen from a battle scene by Bihzad.

کشته شدن کلباد بدست فریبرز
فرود آمد از اسب و بگشاد بند
ز فتراک خویش آن کیانی کمند
همه دشمن شاه خسته جگر

No matter how gory, the slayings in this book are apt to take place in settings of idyllic charm.

Ardashir and the slave girl Gulnar

Ardashir, the founder of the Sasanian dynasty (A.D. 226–652), as a young man found service at Ray with the Parthian king Ardavan, whom he was eventually to overthrow. In Ardavan's palace he was glimpsed by the beautiful Gulnar, the royal favorite and confidante, who immediately fell in love with him. One night, the moon new in the sky, Gulnar in all her finery let herself down by a rope from the battlements of the palace and went to Ardashir's bedside. Awakened, the young man was overcome by her beauty. The lovers' clandestine visits continued for some time, until Ardashir received distressing news from abroad: his grandfather and guardian, Babak, the governor of Fars, had died, appointing his own son, Bahman, in his place. Ardashir, who had expected to inherit the governorship, determined to claim his patrimony by force. Gulnar encouraged him in this decision, and the lovers stole from the palace by night and fled. Ardavan pursued them, but in vain.

516

VERSO This tenderly romantic miniature, according to the inscription on the frieze above the chamber, was painted by Mir Musavvir in 934 A.H. (1527/28).

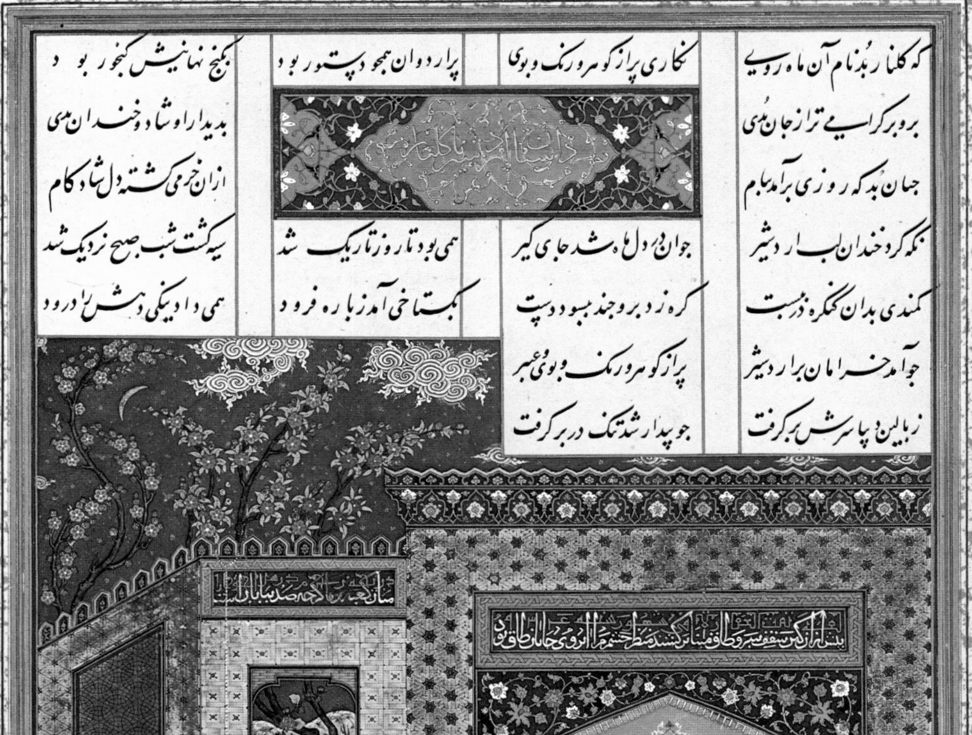

که گلنار بد نام آن ماه روی
نگاری پر از گوهر و رنگ و بوی
پر اردوان همچو دستور بود
بگنج نهانیش گنجور بود
برو بر گرامیتر از جان بدی
بدیدار او شاد و خندان بدی
جهان بد که روزی برآمد ببام
ازان خرمی گشته دل شاد کام
داستان اردشیر با گلنار
نگه کرد خندان لب اردشیر
جوان در دل ماه شد جای گیر
همی بود تا روز تاریک شد
سیه گشت شب صبح نزدیک شد
کمندی بدان کنگره در ببست
گره زد برو چند بسود دست
بگستاخی آمد ز باره فرود
همی داد یکی دهش را درود
چو آمد خرامان بر اردشیر
پر از گوهر و رنگ و بوی عبیر
ز بالین دیبا سرش برگرفت
چو بیدار شد تنگ در برگرفت
نگه کرد برنا بدان خوب روی
بدان برز و بالا و آن روی و موی

Nodding attendants, slack rope, and ecstatic flowers symbolize the tryst. The lovers' slippers are as neatly tucked into the arabesque as they themselves are in the bed in this exquisitely chaste representation of passion.

The story of Haftvad and the worm

Now hear what happened in the poor, hard-working seaside town of Pars. One day the daughter of Haftvad interrupted her spinning to eat an apple. In it she found a worm. Thinking this a good omen, she promised her companions that by the morrow she should have spun wondrous quantities. The girls laughed, but by evening she had already doubled her quantity. To her inquisitive parents she confessed her secret: the magic of the worm. As clever as he was poor, Haftvad gave up his usual work to tend the tiny creature. It grew: its coat became dark as musk and its head and back took on beautiful colors. The whole town prospered. Haftvad was made governor. On a mountain he built a great stronghold with an iron gate. Here the auspicious worm dwelt in a masonry tank. Years passed. On its diet of rice, milk, and honey the worm's limbs grew to the size of an elephant's.

Shah Ardashir, learning of the miraculous creature, sent an army to destroy it. Haftvad defeated the attackers with ease. The shah gathered a greater army and led it in person, but his young heart grew cold at the sight of Haftvad's forces. Later, Ardashir gained some valuable information: the worm was in fact the creation of the div Ahriman and could be conquered only by craft. Disguised as merchants, Ardashir and a picked group begged admittance to the mountain stronghold, the shah announcing that he had so prospered by favor of the worm that he had come to receive its blessing—a statement that convinced everyone of his peaceful intentions. After diverting the worm's attendants with a great feast and strong drink, the conspirators prepared another repast: a brazen pot brimming with boiling lead. Ardashir and two of his men went to the unguarded tank. The worm raised its head and hungrily thrust out its tongue. The metal was poured down its gullet. The agonies of the expiring worm shook the stronghold to its foundations. Killing the attendants, Ardashir signaled to his army, which stormed out from its concealment and assisted in capturing the town. Haftvad and his sons were gibbeted and riddled with arrows.

521

VERSO This miniature, signed in the lower margin by Dust Muhammad, was placed in the book after the rest of the work was completed. An early seventeenth-century version of the subject, probably based on a tracing brought to the Mughal court by Dust Muhammad himself, survives in an album made for Emperor Jahangir. The painter must have gone to the Indian court soon after he completed the album for Prince Bahram Mirza in which he refers to our manuscript (page 16).

صورة دوست محمد

Dust Muhammad's figures, such as these graybeards, tend to be attentuated and disproportionate, and his rocks, containing eyeless, tooth-grinding grotesques, are further evidence that his spirit was troubled.

Haftvad's daughter bites into the fateful apple.

بزد تیر بر پشت آن گور نر
گذر کرد بر گور پیکان و پر

نر و ماده را هر دو بر هم بدوخت
دل لشکر از زخم او برفروخت

ز لشکر هر آن کس که آن زخم دید
بر آن شاخ و یال آفرین گسترید

که چشم بد از فرّ تو دور باد
همه روزگاران تو سور باد

بمردی تو اندر زمانه نوی
که هم شاه و هم پهلوان گوی

وز آنجا برانگیخت شبرنگ شاه
یکی بیشه پیش اندر آمد براه

دو شیر ژیان پیش آن بیشه دید
کمان را بزه کرد و اندر کشید

بزد بر بر و سینهٔ شیر چاک
گذر کرد تا پر و پیکان بخاک

بر ماده شد تیز و بگشاد شست
بر شیر با گردرانش بخست

سپاهش همه خواندند آفرین
که ای نامور شهریار زمین

ندید و نه بیند کس اندر جهان
چو تو شاه بر گاه شاهنشهان

که با تیر پرنی پر تو شیر افکنی
پی کوه خارا ز بن برکنی

Bahram Gur pins the coupling onagers

The Sasanian shah Bahram Gur (reigned 421–438) went hunting one spring day with Ruzbih, his minister, and a thousand cavaliers. The plain was full of wild asses. They were pairing, and the earth was red with the blood of contending bucks. The shah watched as two of the most powerful butted one another. Then, when the victor was covering a jennet, he sent a shaft home to its feathers, pinning the amorous beasts together.

568

RECTO We ascribe this miniature to Mir Sayyid Ali, one of the leading masters of the second generation. Although he was employed as an assistant to Sultan Muhammad and Aqa Mirak, we find him here as a budding young master who has designed and finished his entire composition. Along with Dust Muhammad and Abd al Samad, he eventually left Iran to join the Mughal court of Emperor Humayun. Apparently an unhappy man, he gained a bad reputation for plagiarizing other poets' verses. While still comparatively young, he left India for Mecca, where he died.

In Iranian painting generally and especially in the work of Mir Sayyid Ali we are encouraged to delight in the subplots that surround and occasionally outshine the central subject.

Although this is a youthful work by Mir Sayyid Ali, his technical virtuosity, genius for textile designing, and accuracy of observation are already pronounced.

فراوان بیاراندرون سیم و زر
چه از مشک و عنبر چه از عود تر
ز یاقوت و الماس و از تیغ هند
همه تیغ هندی سراسر پرند

Nushirvan receives an embassy from the king of Hind

One day an embassy from Hind (India) arrived at the court of the Sasanian shah Nushirvan (reigned 531–578), bringing elephants, horsemen, and a thousand camels laden with jewels, gold, silver, musk, aloes, rubies, diamonds, and damascened Hindi scimitars—in short, all the luxuries produced in Qannowj and May. The bales were unpacked before the shah, who listened with keen interest to the ambassador's message, an offer of tribute to Iran if one of Nushirvan's wise men could discover how to play chess, an Indian game. If, however, the Iranians failed to fathom the game, Iran should pay tribute to Hind. Board and pieces were set up before the shah, who inquired about their shape. "They are symbolic," the envoy told him, "of the art of war; and when you know the game you will understand tactics, strategy, and the order of the battlefield." "I will require one week," said the shah. "On the eighth day we shall play willingly."

After the Indians had withdrawn to their quarters, Nushirvan's sages studied the unknown game, moving the pieces in each possible combination. Not even the wisest man could discover the rules until Buzurjmihr, an established master of philosophy, astronomy, medicine, and political theory, brought his intellect to bear on the problem. Afterward, Buzurjmihr invented the game of backgammon, and Nushirvan sent it with a similar embassy to Hind, counteroffering double or nothing. Needless to say, the Barahmans (Brahmans) of India were no match for the sages of Iran.

638

RECTO This large and ambitious miniature, painted in the mid-1530s or even later, can be attributed to Mirza Ali, the son of Sultan Muhammad. Although it is an early work, the artist's favorite types are already present, as are his penchant for still life, his exceptionally fine workmanship, and his tendency to divide crowds into a series of tête-à-têtes.

Gardeners, nurses, and children frequently appear in Mirza Ali's gatherings, and the gatherings themselves are accurate accounts of Safavid life. Mirza Ali's human types, including the fox-faced ambassador and the moon-faced shah (right), are as characteristic of his style as the well-observed still-life details.

فراوان ببار اندرون سیم و زر
چه از مشک و عنبر چه از عود تر
ز یاقوت و الماس و از تیغ هند
همه تیغ هندی سراسر پرند

The assassination of Khosrow Parviz

Khosrow Parviz, one of the last of the Sasanian rulers, known once for his justice, became increasingly unjust over the years. Worse, he surrounded himself with sycophants and tyrants, and countenanced their extortion of the wealth of Iran. He who had been a lamb was now a wolf. Poor people everywhere fled from the woeful conditions in the land. Rebels against the crown released the king's weakling son, Shiruye, from the prison where he had languished in paternal displeasure, and imprisoned Khosrow in palatial splendor with Shirin, his favorite—far too lenient a punishment, according to many of the court dignitaries. These men insisted that Shiruye, now the wearer of the crown, execute his father. The frightened Shiruye acquiesced, with the proviso that his role not become publicly known. Mihr Hormozd, a vile-looking, evil tramp, volunteered for the actual deed, for which he received a purse of gold and a sharp dagger.

When the assassin approached, Khosrow guessed his purpose and, trembling, sent a page for a golden ewer, water, and fresh garments, hoping he would bring help. The naïve boy returned alone. In despair, Khosrow prepared himself for death by putting on the fresh garments and making his confession to God. Mihr Hormozd then silently locked the door, lifted Khosrow's robes, and dispatched him.

742

VERSO

This is the one miniature in the book that can be assigned to Abd al-Samad, on the basis of inscribed pictures by him in Teheran. Most of this artist's work was done at the Mughal court, where, at the behest of Emperor Akbar, he considerably altered his style toward naturalism.

ز پیشش بیامد پرستار چند
چو برسم بدید اندر آمد بباز
یکی چادر نو بسر در کشید
سبک باز شد جامه نو در کشید
جگرگاه شاه جهان بر درید
یکی طشت زرین بر شاه برد
نه گاه سخن بود و هنگام راز
بدان تا رخ جان ستانا زباد
ابا جامه و آبدستان و آب
همی جامه‌ها را بپوشید شاه
بشد مهر هرمزد خنجر بدست
همی کرد خسرو بزردان شتاب
بزمزم همی توبه کرد از گناه
در خانه بر پادشا را ببست
برین گونه گردد جهان تا جهان
همی راز خویش از تو دارد نهان
نمانی همی در سرای سپنج
که خسرو بران گونه بر شد تباه
بایوان شاهی که پابند بود
همی داشت آن انده اندر نهفت
اگر گنج یابی اگر درد و رنج
چو آگاهی آمد ببازار و راه
گرامی ده و پنج فرزند بود
جهاندار چیزی نیارست گفت
ببینید زکردار او جز گزاف
چو خواهی که یابی بداد آفرین
بایوان آن مستمندان شدند
بدانگه که برگشته بد بخت شاه
سخن سنج بی رنج اگر مرد لاف
بی آزاری و راستی برگزین
همان بدگمانان بزندان شدند
بزندان بکشتندشان بیگناه

Peaceful court attendants provide an effective contrast to the cruel scene in a nearby chamber.

It is night. One member of the court has removed his turban to drowse in comfort.

سخن سنج
بی آزاری
همان

Checklist of Paintings in the Houghton *Shah-nameh*

2 VERSO; 3 RECTO
Double-page geometrical frontispiece

7 RECTO
Firdowsi encounters the court poets of Ghazna

10 RECTO
Firdowsi proves his literary talents at the court of Sultan Mahmud

16 RECTO
Dedicatory rosette

16 VERSO
In praise of God and the intellect. (Illuminated page)

18 VERSO
Firdowsi's parable of the ship of Shi'ism

20 VERSO
The court of Gayumars

21 VERSO
Hushang slays the Black Div

22 VERSO
The feast of Sadeh

23 VERSO
Tahmuras defeats the divs

24 VERSO
The court of Jamshid

25 VERSO
The death of King Mirdas

26 VERSO
The snakes of King Zahhak

27 VERSO
Zahhak receives the daughters of Jamshid

28 VERSO
The nightmare of Zahhak

29 VERSO
Zahhak is told his fate

30 VERSO
Zahhak slays Birmayeh

31 VERSO
Kaveh tears Zahhak's scroll

32 VERSO
Faridun orders the ox-head mace

33 VERSO
Faridun crosses the river Dijleh

34 VERSO
Faridun enthroned in the palace of Zahhak as Kundrow blunders in

35 RECTO
The feast of Faridun and Kundrow

36 VERSO
Faridun strikes down Zahhak

37 VERSO
The death of Zahhak

38 VERSO
The court of Faridun

39 VERSO
Faridun's envoy to King Sarv: the first interview

698 VERSO
The envoys of Khosrow Parviz before Caesar

702 RECTO
Kharrad and the weeping statue

707 VERSO
Khosrow Parviz's charge against Bahram Chubineh

708 VERSO
The angel Sorush rescues Khosrow Parviz from a cul-de-sac

715 VERSO
Bahram Chubineh slays the lion-ape

721 VERSO
Bahram Chubineh's sister slays the khaqan's brother

731 RECTO
Barbad, the concealed musician

735 RECTO
Rebels defeat the guard of Khosrow Parviz

742 VERSO
The assassination of Khosrow Parviz

745 VERSO
The coup against Shah Farayn Guraz

Bibliography of Safavid Painting

Akimishkin, O. F., and Ivanov, I. A. A. *Persian Miniatures of the 14th–17th Centuries.* Oriental Miniatures and Calligraphies in Leningrad Collections. edited by U. E. Borshevskii (in Russian). Moscow, 1968.

Arberry, A. J., Minovi, M., and Blochet, E. *The Chester Beatty Library. A catalogue of the Persian Manuscripts and Miniatures.* Edited by J. V. S. Wilkinson. 3 vols. Dublin, 1959–62.

Arnold, Sir Thomas W., and Grohmann, Adolf. *The Islamic Book.* Paris, 1929.

Binyon, Laurence. *The Poems of Nizami.* London, 1928.

Binyon, Laurence, Wilkinson, J. V. S., and Gray, Basil. *Persian Miniature Painting.* London, 1933.

Blochet, Edgard. *Les Enluminures des manuscrits orientaux, turcs, arabes, persans, de la Bibliothèque Nationale.* Paris, 1926.
Les Peintures des manuscrits orientaux de la Bibliothèque Nationale. Paris, 1914–20.
Musulman Painting: XIIth–XVIIth Century. Translated by Cicely M. Binyon. London, 1929.

Coomaraswamy, Ananda K. *Les Miniatures orientales de la collection Goloubew au Museum of Fine Arts de Boston.* Ars Asiatica, XIII, Paris, 1929.

Edhem, Fehmi, and Stchoukine, Ivan. *Les Manuscrits orientaux illustrés de la Bibliothèque de l'Université de Stamboul.* Paris, 1933.

Ettinghausen, Richard. "Some Paintings in Four Istanbul Albums," *Ars Orientalis,* I, 1954, pp. 91–103.

Giuzalian, L., and Diakanov, M. M. *Iranian Miniatures in the Manuscripts of the Shah-nameh from Leningrad Collections.* Moscow, 1935.

Gray, Basil. *Persian Painting.* [New York], 1961.

Grube, Ernst J. *Muslim Miniature Paintings from the XIII to XIX Century from Collections in the United States and Canada.* Venice, 1962.
The Classical Style in Islamic Painting. Edizioni Oriens, 1968.

Guest, Grace D. *Shiraz Painting in the Sixteenth Century.* Washington, D.C., 1949.

Ipsiroglu, M. S. *Saray-Alben. Diez'sche Klebebände aus den Berliner Sammlungen.* Wiesbaden, 1964.
Painting and Culture of the Mongols. New York, 1966.

Ipsiroglu, M. S., and Eyuboglu, S. *Fatih albumuna bir bakiş. Sur l'album du Conquérant.* Istanbul, 1955.

Kerimov, M. *Sultan Muhammad and His School* (in Russian). Moscow, 1970.

Kühnel, Ernst. *Miniaturmalerei im islamischen Orient.* Berlin, 1922.

Loehr, Max. "The Chinese Elements in the Istanbul Miniatures," *Ars Orientalis,* I, 1954, pp. 85–89.

Martin, F. R. *The Miniature Painting and Painters of Persia, India and Turkey from the 8th to the 18th Century.* 2 vols. London, 1912.

Migeon, Gaston. *Manuel d'art Musulman,* I, Paris, 1907.

Muhammad Qazwini, and Bouvat, L. "Deux documents inédits relatifs à Behzâd," *Revue du Monde Musulman,* XXVI, 1914, pp. 146–61.

Paris, Musée des Arts Décoratifs. *Miniatures persanes tirées des collections de Henry d'Allemagne . . . .* Preface by Georges Marteau and Henri Vever. 2 vols. Paris, 1913.

Pope, Arthur Upham. *A Survey of Persian Art from Prehistoric Times to the Present.* 6 vols. Oxford, 1938–39.

Robinson, Basil William. *A Descriptive Catalogue of the Persian Paintings in the Bodleian Library.* Oxford, 1958.
Persian Drawings from the 14th through the 19th Century. New York, 1965.
Persian Miniature Painting from Collections in the British Isles. London, 1967.

Sakisian, Marmenag. *La Miniature persane du XIIe au XVIIe siècle.* Paris, 1929.

Schroeder, Eric. *Persian Miniatures in the Fogg Museum of Art.* Cambridge, Mass., 1942.

Schulz, Philipp Walter. *Die persisch-islamische miniaturmalerei.* 2 vols. Leipzig, 1914.

Stchoukine, Ivan V. *Les peintures des manuscrits safavis de 1502 à 1587.* Paris. 1959.

"Les peintures turcomanes et safavies d'une Khamseh de Nizami achevée à Tabriz en 886/1487," *Ars Asiatiques,* XIV, 1966, pp. 3–16.

Zetterstéen, K. V., and Lamm, C. J. *Mohammed Asafi. The Story of Jamal and Jalal.* Uppsala, 1948.

Zoka, Yahya. "Khawaran Nama," *Honar va Mardom,* 20, 1924, pp. 17–29.